THE SMALL BUSINESS
TURNAROUND GUIDE

THE SMALL BUSINESS TURNAROUND GUIDE

Take Your Business from Troubled to Triumphant

SANDY STEINMAN

NEW YORK

THE SMALL BUSINESS TURNAROUND GUIDE
Take Your Business from Troubled to Triumphant

ISBN 978-1-61448-257-4 paperback
ISBN 978-1-61448-258-1 eBook
Library of Congress Control Number: 2012933817

Morgan James Publishing
The Entrepreneurial Publisher
5 Penn Plaza, 23rd Floor,
New York City, New York 10001
(212) 655-5470 office • (516) 908-4496 fax
www.MorganJamesPublishing.com

Cover Design by:
Rachel Lopez
www.r2cdesign.com

Interior Design by:
Bonnie Bushman
bonnie@caboodlegraphics.com

In an effort to support local communities, raise awareness and funds, Morgan James Publishing donates a percentage of all book sales for the life of each book to Habitat for Humanity Peninsula and Greater Williamsburg.

Get involved today, visit
www.MorganJamesBuilds.com.

To my wife, Mary Kay,
who, being the real change manager in our family,
changed my life forever.

And a special thanks to Amanda Rooker, my copyeditor,
who probably spent twice the time she envisioned in editing
this book, but whose efforts made it infinitely better.

Table of Contents

SPECIAL FREE OFFER!

We recognize that you most likely bought this book because you want to make your Company better. We want you to be successful in this endeavor and so we have the following offers for you that you will find to be incredibly helpful. All you have to do is go to

www.businessturnaroundguide.com/bookoffer

and you will receive a free Profitability Analysis for your business(an $800 value) This Profitability Analysis will let you know where your company stands as compared to companies in your industry and of your size.

Remember, knowledge is power and this particular knowledge is supremely powerful. And as they say in infomercials, There's more. As you begin the journey of taking your Company from troubled to triumphant, you may want a little more help. That is just what we are here to do! We have a special offer for people who bought this book. We will give you a 50% discount of one month of video and phone consulting. That is four two hour sessions and is a $300 savings. Take advantage of this offer now. There is no long term commitment and your satisfaction is guaranteed. You won't be sorry.

Your Business May Be in Trouble if...

... your bank gives you your own NSF stamp and asks that you pre-stamp your checks.

... on payday, your employees get together and write you a check.

... every time you print your financial statements, your printer runs out of red ink.

... your accounts receivable clerk only works half days and your accounts payable clerk has 20 hours of overtime each week.

... your highest customer number is 5.

... you are having a staff meeting, and upon hearing "how's business?" your sales manager bursts into tears.

... your accounts payable department draws straws to see who answers the phone.

... the repo man hauls away your car while you are having lunch with your most important customer.

... you cause an IRS audit flag because they just don't think any company could lose that much money.

... your largest customer asks you, "How long have you been doing business with us—not counting today?"

... your turnaround plan is based upon winning the lottery.

... you have to dig a hole underneath your sales chart to accommodate your trend line.

... you get tons of unsolicited letters from bankruptcy lawyers saying, "We can help you."

... you throw a big celebration party every time you almost break even.

CHAPTER 1

How Funny Is Your Troubled Business?

You may have had a laugh or two from the previous pages. Perhaps this is what comedian Jeff Foxworthy would say if he appeared before a group of troubled businesses owners. The real question is, how funny is *your* business? The quick answer is, not very darn funny. The truth is there is nothing funny about a business that is either failing (as in going down the tubes) or simply failing to meet its potential. You, the business owner, have the real responsibility of stewardship. Just look at the myriad people for whom you are responsible:

- Your family,
- Your employees,
- Your employees' families,
- Your vendors,
- And in some cases, your vendor's families.

And you take that responsibility quite seriously, don't you? It keeps you up at night. It harms your appetite. It takes a genuine toll on your health, both physically and emotionally. It can destroy your most precious relationships.

Up to this point we have not even discussed your biggest responsibility, the person to whom a failing business does the most harm. Who is that person? *It's you!* We are not built to fail, and failure does horrible things to ourselves and our psyches.

So why are you in this predicament? There are many possibilities. Some of those possibilities are:

- Not enough sales
- Not enough cash
- Poor collection of receivables
- Poor communication with your employees
- High employee turnover
- Poor inventory management
- Too much obsolete inventory
- Poor location of business
- Lack of planning
- Lack of leadership skills
- Lack of knowledge in how to manage your business

And we could add even more. The real question is, why haven't you done something about it? Why do you keep doing the same thing and expecting different results? Well, it may be that you just don't know what to do. You may have reached the stage of simply feeling paralyzed, so that you just can't do anything.

The good news is that merely purchasing this book proves you have moved out of the state of denial. That's the first step. Now what are your options?

You can engage a consulting firm to help you determine what should be done. Oh sure, it may cost you $250 to $400 per hour and you may spend in excess of $150,000. You can always take a second mortgage on your house to finance it. Oh, sorry—I forgot, you have already mortgaged your house to finance your business. The fact is, even if you came up with the money, you would still do most of the work.

Or you can find the person who knows the most about your business and, along with the recovery plan set out in this book, you can turn your company around. Now where do you find that person who knows the most about your business? Let me give you a hint. One of my clients once asked me if I knew the definition of a consultant. I told him that I didn't, and he was happy to let me know that the definition of a consultant is someone who borrows your watch and then tells you what time it is. In other words, to find the person who knows most about your business, all you have to do is look in the mirror. That's right! The person who knows most about your business is…YOU! My experience has shown that the client always has the answers.

So look how far you've come. You've identified the one person who knows the most about your business, and you have this dandy guide that will show you how to fix your sick business. You've got it made, right?

Well, not so fast. You are the right person to repair your company, and this book will provide some vital insights. But get ready for a rough ride. The good news is that *you can do it*. If you fully understand that change is hard and are prepared to deal with it, and if you will undertake the actions set out in this book (the same actions that my clients have paid me $400 per hour to have me teach them), then you can make significant positive changes to your company, and by doing so you can drastically improve your life and the lives of those who depend upon you.

Think of yourself as a doctor and your company as a critically ill patient who has come to you because you are a renowned healer and your patient's last hope for survival. You look the patient in the eye and tell him that you are going to do everything within your power to save his life. You know that you are going to have to work day and night to halt the disease that is ravaging his body and then to begin the difficult process of building his body and his immune system up so that he can continue to live a normal, productive life. As you consider what you are about to embark on, you wonder for a moment if all of this time that you are about to invest is really worth it. But the doubt lingers only for a moment, because you know without question that healing this patient will bring you great satisfaction, as well as significant personal rewards. Taking on the task of making your business well is much the same. You know that it is going to be a long and difficult task, but you also know that the rewards that await you outweigh by far the time that you will have invested in the turnaround.

So, you are now the doctor and your company is your patient. In fact, you are in the emergency room treating your critically ill patient. For an ordinary doctor, stabilizing this patient would be a daunting task, but you have no fear. You have been trained (or will be trained through this book) to perform the correct techniques to take your patient from critical to flourishing. Is it going to be easy? Absolutely not. But let's put on our big-boy pants and begin the journey. The first thing that you have to do is *stop the bleeding*. The next chapter will show you the steps you must take immediately to buy yourself enough time to implement the processes that you will read about in this book.

CHAPTER 2

Stop the Bleeding

There are many similarities between a company in trouble and an individual who has been in a horrible accident. The accident victim may have several broken bones, which will require setting and perhaps even surgery, but the first job of the emergency room doctor is to ensure that the victim lives long enough to have those bones set. After all, if his bleeding goes unchecked and he bleeds to death, the broken bones are rather immaterial. So what do we do first for the sick company? We stop the bleeding, because if we don't, we may never have time to implement all of the things that you will learn as you read this book.

We know that accident victims hemorrhage blood, and the emergency room doc must keep that blood from leaking out. Similarly, we know that sick companies hemorrhage cash, and we must stop the cash from leaking out or the company will cease to exist.

As you prepare to take your company from troubled to triumphant, you must first stabilize your company before making changes. So you as the emergency room doctor will have to make some tough decisions—decisions that you may have not been willing to make before.

To stabilize your company, you must personally take control of your cash and find quick ways to improve your cash flow. The three quickest ways to do that are to *reduce your expenses, improve your collections, and negotiate with your vendors.*

Reduce Your Expenses

You must take personal control of your bank account. Nobody should spend a dollar without your approval. Begin expense reductions by looking carefully at your payroll. It is not unusual in turnaround situations for the turnaround manager to eliminate up to 20 percent of the jobs within the company. Is that tough? Of course it is, and the people who remain have to take up the slack, but it is far more preferable than closing the doors. You, as the turnaround manager, will likely find people who can be terminated or furloughed. As you make these decisions, your guiding question should be whether the company can continue to function without the position in question. Who will perform these duties? As you go through the process of eliminating jobs, it is vital that you let the remaining employees know that these changes are necessary if the company is going to survive. Believe me, they won't be surprised. They'll most likely be relieved by the fact that you are actually taking some action.

These actions are often particularly difficult for family-owned businesses that have layers of family on the payroll. You may have to slash family members' jobs just like you would any other job. Remember, the key is to buy yourself some time so you can fix your company.

Don't assume that all of the expense savings comes from payroll. Examine every expense. I can promise you that you will find costs that are not necessary to your company's survival and, in fact, are detrimental at this time. Pay particular attention to various memberships and subscriptions that you have set up to be automatically deducted from your bank account or automatically charged to your credit card. Many of these costs renew automatically and some can be easily eliminated. Remember that every dollar you save increases your chances of survival.

One change I often see owners make is to reduce or completely eliminate their salaries. *Do not do this!* You, as an owner, are taking all of the risks, and you are entitled to fair compensation. In fact, many times I will suggest to owners in a turnaround situation to give themselves a raise if they have been shortchanging themselves.

Improve Your Collections

Chances are you have a fair amount of cash tied up in accounts receivable. You must convert those older receivables to cash. While a later section of this book also deals with collections, you have to take action now. You can implement effective collection procedures once you have created some breathing room for your company. Again, you are going to have to make some tough decisions. Take an aging of your receivables and identify the customers who are seriously delinquent. You, as the owner, must call them and demand your money. Be relentless. Call after hours if necessary. Call the owners of your customers at home if you have to. Just keep the pressure on your slow-paying customers. Customers who refuse to pay or refuse to create some type of payment arrangement will have to be put on credit hold and sold only on a COD basis. Could you lose some customers during this process? Sure, but what good is a non-paying customer? While you are in triage mode, you have to be ruthless. I had a client in the construction industry with revenues of about $7,000,000 annually. He told me that he was going to have to close his doors because he was running out of cash. His real problem was that he had a very large customer who was a publicly held general contractor for whom he had done some large jobs. This customer owed him over $750,000. This entire amount was delinquent and the GC told him they didn't know when he would pay. It was time to be ruthless. I picked up the telephone and called the CEO of the company. I explained the situation to him and told him that in twenty-four hours we were going to call a press conference to announce that this poor minority business owner was being forced to close his doors and put forty employees on the street because this large mega-company didn't pay him. I didn't yell and I wasn't out of control. In fact, I was so much in control that the CEO believed I was crazy enough to do what I promised. He asked if I could delay the press conference by a day and promised he would get back to me within twenty-four hours. I agreed to that timetable. Within twenty-four hours he called and agreed to a payment plan that, over a three-week period, would have my client paid in full. Being ruthless can work. Pick your battles and remember that your goal is to collect your money and buy time to fix your company. You are in a war, and your daily battle is to collect the cash that you need to keep your business running.

Negotiate Payments with Vendors

The next thing that you have to do is to begin negotiating payments with your vendors. Come on, they already know you are struggling because you are getting lots of collection calls from them. Of course, when they call you, you find ways to pay them, because that is what responsible companies do. They pay their bills. But the truth is that responsible *and solvent* companies pay their bills in a timely manner, and solvent just does not describe you—yet. So what are you going to do? You are going to do the same things that companies like Amazon have done. You are going to talk to your suppliers, explain the situation to them, and work out a plan to delay your payments. You might ask, how is this going to help me long term? Well, let's assume that your monthly non-payroll costs are $350,000. If you work out a thirty-day delay in payments, you have created for yourself a thirty-day, interest-free permanent loan. Amazon virtually doubled its cash flow by utilizing that strategy. And the delay doesn't have to be a lot of days, but you do need to negotiate it up front. Remember, you must make vendors understand there is no alternative; you need this concession to survive and stabilize. Why would they agree to it? It's a lot better for them than taking pennies on the dollar in bankruptcy court.

Now you are starting to put together a battle plan. You have reduced your payroll and other costs. You have accelerated your collections. You have reached an agreement with your suppliers to delay payments. All of these actions spell C-A-S-H and will help buy you the time you need to do the things you will learn in the following chapters, which will take you some time to implement but will help you get your company back on solid footing.

CHAPTER 3

The Process of Change

In his book *The Prince,* Niccolo Machiavelli writes, "It ought to be remembered that there is nothing more difficult to take in hand, more perilous to conduct, or more uncertain in its success, than to take the lead in the introduction of a new order of things, because the innovator has for enemies all those who have done well under the old conditions and only lukewarm defenders among those who may do well under the new."[1]

The process of dealing with change has not changed since Machiavelli's time. But there's another truism that also hasn't changed since Machiavelli's time: Knowledge is power. In my opinion, the best body of knowledge on the subject of change is Stephen R. Covey's *The Four Disciplines of Execution.*[2] Mastering the four disciplines of execution will go a long way in helping you manage the process

1   Niccolo Machiavelli, *The Prince,* trans. William K. Marriott (Wasteland Classics, 2010), p. 26.
2   Stephen R. Covey, *The Four Disciplines of Execution* (Covey, 2004). A portion of this chapter is adapted from the audio book version of this work and is used here by permission. I certainly recommend any of Franklin Covey's products.

of change. But before we get into those disciplines, let's learn more about why execution can be so difficult to begin with.

The Tyranny of the Urgent

In order to begin any kind of large-scale change strategy, it's important to understand that *developing* strategies and *executing* strategies are two entirely different issues. Developing strategies typically involves only one person: the leader. But executing strategies means not only changing the leader's behavior, but changing a lot of other people's behavior. And the more the leader is in love with the strategy, the more likely it is that he will screw up the execution, because he will underestimate the difficulty in getting it done.

What makes execution so difficult? In a word: multitasking. It is just plain hard to focus because there are so many things to get done in a day. Most people don't know how to filter through all of their multiple priorities to ensure that they accomplish their most important priorities.

We have trouble executing because there is an inherent conflict between the forces of the *whirlwind* (that is, your day job, which encompasses everything that has to happen in your business every day to maintain your operation) and the *goals* that have to be accomplished. Even if you did not have any goals, would our people still be busy every day? Of course they would. Just look at the divergent nature of the whirlwind and the nature of the goals. The nature of the whirlwind is urgent; the nature of the goals is important. When there is a conflict between the important and the urgent, what wins? Urgent—every time!

Why is that a truism? Because the bad results that you get from ignoring the whirlwind are more immediate than the bad results that you get from ignoring the goals.

It's not that our leaders are bad or defiant; it's that they are busy with the "real work." That is the reality when we present new, exciting goals. You will hear things like, "Yeah, I like the sound of the idea, but I've got to get back to the real work." So the fundamental challenge in execution is not merely achieving the goal. The challenge is achieving the goal in the midst of the whirlwind.

Specifically, Covey has identified four ways execution typically breaks down in the whirlwind of daily work:

1. People don't know what the goals are.
2. The goal or goals are not translated into day-to-day activities.

3. People on teams aren't keeping score. There is no way for them to know whether or not they are on track.

4. People on teams aren't held accountable for their goals, either to each other or to the company.

To address each of these typical obstacles and to help us with execution in the midst of the whirlwind, we are going to look at four disciplines of execution. Disciplines are not hard to *think about,* but they are hard *to do.* These are principles that are unalterable, in that you can ignore them, but they will still be there to bury you if you don't deal with them. And they are sequential, in that if you don't do well with the first discipline, you won't do well with disciplines two through four. Now that you've been warned, let's explore the disciplines.

Discipline 1: Focus on the Wildly Important

Discipline 1 is to focus on the *wildly important.* Wildly important goals are the few goals outside of the whirlwind that makes achieving any other goal inconsequential. If a team has three wildly important goals, we have a pretty fair chance of accomplishing them. But if we have four to ten goals, our chances go down. This is called the law of diminishing returns.

If you tell people to focus on the wildly important goals but don't acknowledge the whirlwind, the team is going to rebel and turn you off. Remember, I said *acknowledge* the whirlwind—not focus on it. We have to focus on the things outside the whirlwind, the things that are going to move the company forward. Most leaders make the mistake of not differentiating between the goal and the whirlwind. The goals of today may well become part of the whirlwind tomorrow.

Narrow the focus so that it is truly on the wildly important. Lance Armstrong, after he recovered from cancer, decided that his wildly important goal was to once again win the Tour de France. He dropped out of all other competitions to train for the tour so he could win that most coveted of all bicycle races.

So the wildly important goal would be defined as *great,* while the rest of the goals are defined as *good.* It is hard to say no to good things, but sometimes you have to say no to the good to accomplish the great.

Discipline 1 must have a clear finish line. In other words, just saying that we have to get from X to Y is not enough. The real question is when. That defines the finish line.

An example of this is President Eisenhower's response when Russia first developed Sputnik and satellites. His mantra was that the United States would lead the way into space. Nice slogan, but it was ineffective. There was just no accountability. *When* would the United States lead the way into space? A more effective goal was set when President Kennedy said, "We will put a man on the moon by the end of the decade." Looking back, knowing that our BlackBerries have more than a hundred times the memory of the Saturn 5 rocket, we probably had no business expecting to be on the moon by the end of the 1960s. But the goal had a clear finish line with focus and accountability, and as a result it was effective. When accountability went up, so did morale around the space program, and this was a very important phenomenon. Kennedy also said that the United States was not going to pursue any other goals in the meantime, even good goals. He obviously knew that the enemy of the great is the good.

Discipline 2: Act on the Lead Measure

After you've narrowed your focus to the wildly important, we should begin thinking about the *lag measure* and the *lead measure*. The lag measure measures the achievement of the goal. It is easy to measure, but difficult to influence. For example, if the goal is weight loss, the lag measure is how much weight you lose—easy to measure, but harder to influence because it takes self-discipline. In contrast, the lead measure has two characteristics: 1) it is predictive, meaning that if the lead measure moves, the goal or lag measure will move, and 2) it is influenceable, which means that we can get our hands around it and control it. The lead measures for our example would be the calories we take in and the calories we burn. After all, if your calorie intake meets your goal, and the number of calories you burn meets your goal, it is predictive that you will lose weight. For an accurate lead measure, it is mandatory that both characteristics be present. Sometimes you can have a measure that is predictive but you have no control over it. That won't work.

One caution here: People make the mistake of always focusing on the lag measure because 1) it is so important and 2) it is so easy to get. If I have scales in my bathroom, it sure is easy to check my weight. The problem is that while I am standing on the scale, I have no idea how many calories I have ingested that day and how many I have burned. For example, one construction company had a problem with on-the-job accidents. They set up the reduction of incidents as the wildly important goal. The lag measure was the incident report, and the lead measure was wearing the protective equipment. The bet was, if we wear the eight articles of safety equipment, accidents would go down.

The problem is that we can't go to the computer and see how we did wearing safety equipment. What do we have to do? Go observe it. See if the men are wearing the equipment. Many organizations come close to cracking the code, and then they retreat, saying, "Oh, we can't measure that; it's too hard." Sure, it's only the wildly important goal, but it's too hard. It was true that observing it was not easy. Every day one of their foreman had to leave their crew—their whirlwind— and go measure whether or not the equipment was being worn. Interestingly, that is never going to feel urgent, which is a characteristic of a lead measure. It will be important but never urgent. The very things that will drive execution will never feel urgent. They are just the most important things. But measuring the right lead measures has an amazing effect on morale, because when the team members understand exactly how they contribute to the wildly important goals of the company, they totally buy in.

Discipline 3: Keep a Compelling Scoreboard

People play differently when score is being kept. Even from a distance, you can tell if a group of kids playing basketball is keeping score by their intensity, energy, shot selection, and teamwork.

A compelling scoreboard does not just mean a group of numbers on the wall; people will disengage if they don't understand how the score is kept or if they feel they can't influence the score. The scoreboard has to tell them if they are winning, it must be simple and updatable, and it must be a player's scoreboard, not a coach's scoreboard. And the scoreboard must show the players both the lead and the lag measures. We often send people to work as if we're sending them to bowl through a curtain. They are doing it blind. They don't know how they are doing, they can't see the goal, and they're not having fun. But we tell them, "We are paying you, aren't we? And you like bowling, don't you?" People would rather be engaged in an effort that they understand than bowl through a curtain. The team has to appreciate the scoreboard, or it is no good and it won't work.

Discipline 4: Create a Cadence of Accountability

To create a cadence of accountability, set up a twenty-minute meeting in which the team makes a quick report of what they have done in the last week to move the lead measure, and then describes what they are going to do this week to move the scoreboard. What they did last week, and what they are going to do this week. Remember, these are things that they come up with by themselves. We're not telling them what to do; they are telling us what they are going to do. That is now a motivated team. This is referred to as "just-in-time" planning. We plan every week what we are going to do. This level of detail could not be part of the strategic plan, which is a much longer-range process.

If the lead measure goes up and the lag stays constant, what does that tell us? We have a bad lag measure, and we must revise it.

Now let's get going! Every day that you delay in executing the needed changes will cost you thousands of dollars that you can never recover.

CHAPTER 4

The Physical Examination

The first step that every doctor takes when diagnosing a patient's illness is a thorough physical examination, which always begins with a history of the patient's health and lifestyle. And so it is with a healer of sick businesses. Of course, you are not going to have to wear one of those funny gowns with an opening in the back. (Unless you want to, of course, and that might mean you have another problem altogether.)

The following questions create the basis for taking a sick company's history and completing the physical examination. They must be answered with significant thought and with total honesty (no matter how painful the answer may be). You will find that this is not easy, because you are both asking and answering the questions. Some of the questions will result in further introspection. For example, one of the questions requires you to note what your sales are, what they could be, and what they should be. I always follow up with the question, "Why do you think your sales are not what they should be?"

It is imperative that when you answer these questions, you really dig down within yourself for the answers as to why you are not achieving what you should be achieving in each of these areas. If you are fortunate enough to have someone you trust who will challenge you to be truthful and thoughtful, you may find it helpful to have that individual conduct the interview and challenge you when necessary. I would not recommend that you use one of your employees to act as interviewer, because some of the questions require you to critically evaluate your key employees. This interview should be carried out just as it would if I were sitting in front of you asking you the questions. I can assure you that I would not allow you to take the easy way out with any of the answers.

The physical examination is our starting point. Go ahead—write your answers in the book.

Business Health History and Physical Exam

Corporate

1. When did you start up the company? Write a brief description of the company's history. Do you believe that the company has achieved the goals that you originally set out for it? If not, why not?

   _____

   _____

   _____

   _____

2. Are all officers associated with the business on a full-time basis, or do they have other business interests? If they do have other interests, how does it affect the company?

   _____

   _____

_____

_____

_____

3. Is there a general manager? If something breaks down and an emergency decision is necessary, how is the decision made?

_____

_____

4. How much help can you count on from each of the following outside advisors?

CPA _____

LAWYER _____

BANKER _____

IT _____

OTHER _____

5. How often do your directors meet to discuss the performance of the company? If the answer is rarely or never, why not? How can you resolve this issue?

_____

_____

_____

_____

6. Are there any affiliated or subsidiary companies? If the answer is yes, do you track the financial results for each affiliate or subsidiary company? Does each affiliate or subsidiary carry its own weight financially? How do you know?

    _____

    _____

    _____

    _____

Managerial Finance

7. What are your current annual sales? What were they last year? The year before? What changes have you made in response to rising or falling sales?

    _____

    _____

    _____

    _____

    _____

8. What should sales be? What could sales be? Why aren't they what they could be? What is preventing you from moving sales to what they could be?

    _____

    _____

_____

_____

_____

_____

9. What volume is required to break even? If you don't know, why don't you know? Do you know how to calculate "break even"?

_____

_____

10. What is your current amount of working capital? Is your cash flow positive? If not, why not? What kind of cash management system do you currently use? If you don't use one, why not? Do you know what your cash position will be four weeks from now? If the answer is no, why not?

_____

_____

11. What was your profit before taxes last year? What was it two years ago? How about three years ago? Is that what you planned? Are you satisfied with that? Why is it up or down?

_____

_____

_____

_____

12. What should the profit be? What will it be this year? If the profit is not what it should be, why not? Do you have targets or budgets to make sure you achieve this?

_____

_____

_____

13. What is your current gross profit? Last year? What should it be? If the gross profit is not what it should be, why not?

_____

_____

14. How often do you receive profit and loss (P&L) statements, and who prepares them? If you do not receive P&-L statements monthly, what can you do to ensure that you start receiving them monthly?

_____

_____

_____

15. Describe your operations in writing. What does your product line consist of? Are your financial statements departmentalized into profit or cost centers to show your bottom line results in each area? If the answer is no, how do you know whether or not each area is profitable?

_____

_____

_____

_____

_____

_____

16. Who is in charge of receivables? What is the current amount of accounts receivable? Who is responsible for reducing receivables? Do you know how many days of sales there are in accounts receivable? If the answer is no, why not?

_____

_____

_____

_____

17. What are your terms? What systems do you have in place to track your receivables?

_____

_____

_____

_____

_____

18. From how many vendors do you currently buy? Do you take advantage of purchase discounts? How much could you save by doing so?

_____

_____

_____

_____

19. Do you measure the performance of your suppliers? Are you satisfied with their performance? Are you getting three new bids twice a year from each supplier?

_____

_____

_____

_____

20. Who is in charge of accounts payable? What is your current amount of accounts payable? What are the terms your suppliers expect? What is the average age of your payables? What systems do you have to schedule your payables? When is the last time you audited your paid invoices for overpayments and duplicate payments?

_____

_____

_____

_____

21. What are your plans for the next six months? The next year? The next three to five years? Longer time? Is the plan in writing? If not, why not?

_____

_____

_____

_____

22. How many individual sales orders (jobs, meals, etc.) do you process during each month? What do you sell the most of and why?

_____

_____

_____

_____

23. Who are your major customers? How did they find out about you? Have you ever advertised or done promotions? How did they work? What were you specifically hoping to accomplish? Do any one of your customers make up 25 percent or more of your business? If the answer is yes, what are your plans to diminish the risk inherent in having one customer that is so important?

_____

_____

_____

_____

24. How broad is the geographical area you service? What are your strongest and weakest geographical areas? Why? How do you distribute your products? What percentage of your market do you control?

_____

_____

_____

_____

25. How many salespeople do you employ? Are they paid on some type of a commission plan? If not, why not? Are you satisfied with their performance? If not, why not?

_____

_____

_____

_____

26. How do you determine the productivity of your salespeople? What reports and controls do you utilize?

_____

_____

_____

_____

27. Who is your main competition? What is their share of market relative to yours? What do they do well? What is their profit margin compared to yours?

Competitor	Share of Market	% Margin

28. What do you believe that the future trends in your industry will be? If you believe the future is bright, what will you do to take advantage of the opportunity? If you believe the future is problematic, what will you do to make sure you survive?

_____

_____

_____

_____

Production and Manufacturing

29. How much more could you produce with your current facilities and personnel? Are you at 80 percent of capacity? If you are not at 80 percent, what must you do to move you toward that goal? If you are approaching full capacity, what are your options to create additional capacity? Do you have the option of second and third shifts?

_____

_____

_____

_____

30. How do you schedule production runs? How do you control costs and ensure quality of output?

_____

_____

_____

_____

31. Are you funding depreciation? How do you plan for—and analyze—the feasibility of capital expenditures?

_____

_____

_____

_____

Computerization

32. Are you computerized? Why or why not? If yes, when did you buy your system? What did you hope it would do for you? How much did you spend on it?

_____

_____

_____

_____

33. What management reports do you get from the computer (or otherwise), and how often do you receive them?

General Ledger_____ Inventory Control _____

Chart of Accounts _____ Production Scheduling_____

A/R Aging _____ Material Variance Report _____

A/P Aging _____ Labor Variance Report _____

Cash Flow Statement _____ Overhead Variance Report _____

P&L Statement _____ Departmental Variance _____

Budget to Actual _____ Sales Performance (product)_____

Other_____ Sales Performance (territory) _____

Other_____ Sales Performance (salesperson) _____

34. Why don't you get all the information that you need?

_____

_____

_____

_____

Bank Relationship/Owner Compensation

35. Do you now have, or have you ever had, financial difficulties?

_____

_____

_____

36. How much do you currently owe? Do you have an established credit line? What is the maximum amount that you can borrow? Why can't you borrow more?

_____

_____

_____

37. What would you do with an extra $200,000?

_____

_____

_____

38. Have you ever leveraged your receivables or inventory?

_____

_____

_____

_____

39. What is your personal compensation? Are you satisfied with it? What is your net worth? If your business does cash transactions, are you including those transactions in gross sales? If you are not reporting it in gross sales, do you know what those cash transactions amount to?

_____

_____

_____

Personnel

40. How many employees do you currently have? Is this expanding or contracting? Why? Do you have all of the key employees that you need?

Department	Number of Employees
Sales	
Administrative	
Production	
Marketing	
Distribution	
Other	

41. What is your employee turnover rate? What does it cost you to hire and train a new employee?

_____

_____

_____

_____

42. Do you have a pay-for-performance plan for all employees? If not, why not?

_____

_____

_____

_____

43. How much has the pay-for-performance plan improved productivity in the business?

_____

_____

_____

_____

Inventory Control

44. What is the current amount of inventory? Do you have a perpetual or periodic system? Do you know how fast all items are turning and at what margins?

_____

_____

_____

45. Do you have inventory control procedures? How are items withdrawn? Is the area secured?

_____

_____

_____

_____

46. Have there ever been any problems with theft of inventory?

_____

_____

_____

_____

Product/Job Costing

47. What are your most profitable products? If you don't know your profitability by product line, how do you know on which products to focus? What systems do you have to monitor and control your product costs?

_____

_____

_____

_____

48. How do you allocate overhead to your product lines/jobs? How do you track labor and materials costs for each product line/job?

_____

_____

_____

_____

Organization

49. How is your company organized? List your key people. What are their duties and incomes?

_____

_____

_____

_____

50. What are your key employees' strengths and weaknesses? Are you satisfied with their performance? How do you rate it on a scale of 1 to 10? If any of them is not a 9 or 10, do you have an action plan to move them to a 9 or 10?

_____

_____

_____

_____

51. Would you rehire each of your key employees? If not, what are your plans to replace them? How will you determine who should be hired?

_____

_____

_____

_____

52. How often do you hold formal, structured meetings with key personnel? If the answer is not at least once a week, why not?

_____

_____

_____

_____

53. What would you consider your most urgent problem? (An urgent problem is a problem that, if not corrected at once, will cause something very bad to happen.)

_____

_____

_____

_____

54. What would you consider your most important problem? (An important problem is a problem that, when left unresolved, will become an urgent problem.)

_____

_____

_____

_____

55. If you had a magic wand and could make any changes in your company you want by simply waving it, what would your company look like today?

_____

_____

_____

Okay, you can get dressed now. The actual physical exam is over. Oh, and one more thing. Please hold your examination gown together in the back as you go to get dressed.

CHAPTER 5

Examine Your Test Results

O kay, you have now completed your business health history and physical exam. Take a deep breath. That wasn't easy. But just as a physician would do after completing a physical exam, it is time to examine some of your results and determine if your answers lead us to any conclusions, or at least to some areas for further discussion.

1. If your company hasn't met its goals, be honest about the reasons why. And, by the way, the mere fact that you are reading this book tells us that you haven't met your goals for the company—after all, nobody starts a business with plans to have a sick company. In hindsight, what could you have done differently that might have yielded better results? What steps can you take now to improve the situation?

2. Sometimes businesses have part-time officers and owners who, for various reasons, do not devote full-time effort to the business. Sometimes these divided interests are a bit like trying to be "partially pregnant." It

just doesn't work. If this is true in your case, it's time to unravel this situation now.

4. & 5. Outside advisors are vital. Not just bean counters, who are with you as long as you are making deposits but run for the hills if you need a loan, but people whom you can count on to back you up and give you good advice. If you are like most small companies, you don't have a board of directors. And if your company is troubled, fear of potential personal liability may make it difficult to convince someone to sit on your board. One of the companies that I turned around had a board of advisors, and that worked well. This board was comprised of people from a variety of disciplines who were genuinely committed to helping this company. They did not do it for money; they did it because they cared about the owner and wanted to see him have a healthy company. The board met monthly and helped to hold the owner accountable for making the changes that he had agreed to implement.

6. If there are affiliated companies, it is important that each company carry its own weight financially. One segment of the operation cannot be allowed to bring another segment down.

7. Sales should always be on a positive track. Simple inflation mandates that. It is important that you analyze your sales carefully and determine if your sales increase is caused by higher prices alone, or if you actually have experienced an increase in the number of sales transactions. Whether your sales are rising or falling, it is important to analyze the changes you have made in response to your sales condition.

   You must respond to changing sales conditions. If sales are down, you must make changes to stop the slide. This may mean examining your sales process, your sales compensation process, your marketing, your advertising, and even your customers' perception of you. If you are fortunate enough to find yourself in a situation in which sales are up, you want to be sure that you are taking full advantage of the positive market conditions that exist and that you are optimizing all of your sales opportunities.

8. It is extremely important to be honest when answering this question. If sales are not what they should be, you must be clear as to what is preventing you from moving sales to the appropriate level. I had a client several years ago who told me that his sales were about 25 percent of

what they could be, given his physical facility. Once we identified the immediate problems and developed solutions, it was a three-year journey to achieve the level of "should be." In my experience, the problems range from the owner not knowing that he had the wrong people in the sales organization to the owner not wanting to make the necessary changes in paying the sales staff. People who are responsible for generating sales should always, always be paid on some sort of a commission basis. We will discuss the principles of developing good commission plans in chapter 14, "Pay Your Way to Recovery."

9. As a business owner, it is crucial to know how much revenue you have to produce to break even. Many owners I have met don't have any idea what their break-even is. Even more disturbing is that they are almost afraid to discover what it is. Remember, knowledge is power. Even if the news is not good, once you know what you need to break even, you can begin to take action to achieve that level. If you will e-mail me at freestuff@ profitabilitypartners.com, I will be happy to send you the calculation.

10. If you don't have a good handle on your cash, you are not alone. Very few of the business owners I have worked with had any idea of what their working capital was, and they rarely knew whether or not their cash flow was negative or positive. Worse yet, most had not even prepared even a short-term cash forecast. You should always know what your cash is going to look like for the next six to eight weeks. If you don't know where the shortfalls are going to occur, you can't take actions to prevent or mitigate those shortfalls. Even if the action involves borrowing money to get you past the shortfall. Believe me, it is much easier to explain to your banker that you foresee a cash shortage in four weeks and will need some help than to ask your banker for help once you are overdrawn. Just e-mail me at freestuff@profitabilitypartners.com, and I will send you the cash plan worksheet.

11. If you can't give an honest appraisal of why your profits are either up or down over the past few years, that means that you have decided to simply react to the forces affecting your operations rather than taking a proactive approach. Go back and review what happened. History teaches us great lessons. Has your gross margin decreased? What caused it? What do you need to do to correct the problem? What has happened to your expenses? Is it time to do a little zero-based budgeting? For those of you

who may not understand zero-based budgeting, it is a process in which you assume you have no overhead costs and then set about to determine what expenses are required to support your revenue and margin plan. Any expense that is not required to support those plans is not budgeted.

12. Again, I assume that because you are participating in this process, your profit does not satisfy you. Be honest with yourself. Why is your profit not meeting your expectations? Is your product or service competitive? Are you producing enough gross margin to get you to profitability? Are your expenses in line with your revenues? Are your employees committed to your plan? Do you have an operating plan? If I were a betting person, I would guess that the answer is a resounding "no!" Should you have an operating plan? You bet! In my consulting practice, I learned that companies with operating plans consistently outperform companies without operating plans. Think about it. The reason is simple. Attempting to operate a business without a clear, concise plan to meet your goals is just like trying to go on an automobile trip without a map. We will discuss the principles involved in creating a plan in chapter 8, "Plan Your Recovery."

13. If your gross profit is not what it should be, you must clearly identify the cause. There is no room for sugar-coating the problem here. You have to look at every piece of the puzzle. Are you controlling the costs of manufacturing your product or providing your service? If you are manufacturing your product, are you utilizing lean manufacturing theories? Are you selling your product or service for an adequate price that will allow you to cover direct costs and overhead while providing you with sufficient profitability?

Once I had a client who was thoroughly confused. He was losing money and didn't know why. The company had been in business for over forty years and had a terrific history, but over the previous three years it had lost nearly $1,000,000 on revenues of about $7,000,000 per year. Worse yet, the losses were increasing. My client told me that employees were working their tails off, successfully obtaining new business, and completing projects on time, and yet, as revenues grew, so did their losses. On the second day of the project, I discovered through an analysis of fully burdened labor costs that they just were not charging a high enough hourly rate to cover their costs. In other words, the more they sold, the more they lost. Once they adjusted the hourly rate, profits increased immediately. And customers were not lost because of higher bidding rates. In the first year of operating at the correct prices, the company earned over $500,000 and was well on the way to a million-dollar profit. All it took was knowledge. You can do the same thing. I will teach you how. One of the first things that you must do is to use the same process that I used on that second day and determine what you have to charge per hour to cover your overhead. If you will e-mail me at freestuff@profitabilitypartners.com, I will e-mail you the fully burdened labor cost worksheet along with instructions for its use.

14. The monthly financial statement is crucial. Many clients have told me during the opening interview they either don't receive financial statements until the end of the year, or if they do receive financial statements, they receive them significantly after the end of the month (sometimes even months after the end of the reporting month). You must do whatever is necessary to ensure that you receive this valuable information no later than ten working days after the previous month's end. These financial statements are not just pieces of paper with a lot of numbers on them. (Go ahead. Admit it. That's what you think they are.)

    The truth is that these statements—the balance sheet, the income statement, and the statement of source and application of cash—contain vital information that you must be prepared to act upon immediately. Of course, if you get them after that ten-day window, they do become just pieces of paper with numbers on them, because the information is no longer actionable. To be actionable, these statements should be compared to your operating plan. (We will discuss this plan a little later.) But don't get the statements and just go into your office, close the door, and try to decipher them. Review them with a trusted advisor or at your monthly board of advisors' meeting, particularly with someone who will challenge you and make you dig deep down within yourself to decide what changes should be made.

15. I can't overemphasize how important it is to know your product-line profitability. I have seen countless clients who have diverse product lines but don't have the foggiest idea as to which product lines are profitable and which are not. Many times they were focused on increasing the sales in product lines that were money losers.

16. and 17. If you aren't firmly in control of your accounts receivable, you are missing the boat. Think about it. Let's say that you've done everything right up to this point. You have driven sales, maximized your gross margin—but uh-oh, where is your cash? It is in accounts receivable. You must have one individual responsible for collecting your receivables, and that person must use the correct process in collecting those receivables. Too many "collectors" get on the phone and say something like, "Hi, this is Betsy from XYZ Company and, uh, like, I noticed that, uh, you owed us some money, and, uh, I was hoping that you could send it in soon." Most of the time this approach results in the response, "Well, we don't have the money right now." Which leaves poor Betsy to say, "Okay, I'll check with you next week." Your collector must use the correct process and must always remember that once the product is sold, the money no longer belongs to the customer, it belongs to you. Your collector is not asking your customers for their money, but instead he is asking them to remit your money.

Remember, no matter how skilled you may be in executing the sale, the transaction is not complete until the money has been collected. You will find my recommended collection process in chapter 15, "Collect Your Way to Recovery." Additionally, too many business owners are content to receive a printout that contains an aging of accounts receivable. You must know how many days of sales you have in your receivables. You must have a goal of how many days' sales in receivables you will accept and what actions you will take if you do not achieve the goal. Please e-mail me at freestuff@profitabilitypartners.com, and I will be happy to send you a spreadsheet that will allow you to calculate the number of days of sales in your accounts receivable.

18. Calculating the value of discounts is just pure dollars and sense. If there are discounts you are not using, it is important to calculate the value and set an immediate goal of taking advantage of those discount opportunities. Take a look at what your interest cost would be if you were to borrow the money (if you can) to take advantage of the discounts.

19 It is vital that you measure the performance of your suppliers. I have seen cases again and again where customers accepted the product of one supplier much more enthusiastically than that of another supplier. Yet the business owner seemed oblivious to the real-world situation. Yes, loyalty

is still alive and well today, but it is always in your best interest to get three bids before deciding on a supplier. While you may not want to change suppliers, you at least want to keep your current supplier honest and competitive.

I recently had a client who was truly loyal to his suppliers. He had dealt with the same supplier of sheet-metal rolls for fifteen years. I encouraged the purchasing manager to get competing bids on fifteen-gauge rolls. They received a bid that was $40 a roll less than what they were currently paying—and they were buying over 1,500 rolls each year! When they told their current supplier about the competing quote, the supplier met the new price with no questions asked. One telephone call resulted in a savings of over $60,000 annually that went right to the bottom line. Remember, this businessman had been dealing with the same company for fifteen years. He had probably left nearly a million dollars on the table over those years. Every one percent you can save goes right to the bottom line.

20. If you are experiencing financial difficulties, we can assume that you are not paying your vendors on a current basis. Two things must be done in this case. First, you must communicate with your vendors on a regular basis. Your communication must be frequent and honest, and your estimate of when payments will be made must be conservative. The worst thing that you can do is to promise something that you cannot deliver on. Now would be a great time to remember the adage "underpromise and overdeliver." Next, you would be amazed how many duplicate payments and overpayments occur on a regular basis. There are companies who make their living auditing accounts-payable payments and receiving their compensation based upon what they recover for companies. When I was CFO for a medium-sized retailer, one of these companies recovered well over $100,000.

21. You simply must know where you are going and have a written plan to get there. Yes, it takes time, and I know that it feels like you are under attack and fighting fires, but much of that is because of your lack of planning. This is called taking care of business. You will find much more about this subject in chapter 8, "Plan Your Recovery."

22. It's amazing, but there are many business owners who have no idea what their leading product seller is and, more importantly, why they

sell more of one product than another. Take time to determine which product(s) are your bestsellers, find out why, and maximize this advantage. Talk to your customers. This type of knowledge is what survival is based on.

23. When you spend money on advertising and promotion, you must find ways to measure the productivity of your investment. This will be much more difficult to accomplish if your advertising is institutional rather than product-specific. Make every attempt to discover what advertising works and what does not work. A very simple process is to ask a prospect how he or she found you. You will get a variety of answers that range from the Yellow Pages to the Internet to perhaps even direct mail, if you have utilized that. The important thing is to try to determine your ROI on the advertising money you spend.

Now let's get to the really important piece of this puzzle. If you determined that more than 25 percent or more of your business is coming from one customer, let me assure you that you are in grave danger. Sure, it's easy to provide products and services to one large customer. You know what they want. There are great efficiencies. But what happens when the customer takes their business elsewhere? And believe me, they always go away. Nothing is forever.

I had a client in the janitorial supply business who, before he came to me, had a customer whose revenue comprised over 35 percent of his company's business. Let me tell you, his company earned a lot of money from this customer. The problem was that they had no plan for the future. Nor was there a strategy in place for recovery if the customer ever went away. Guess what happened? The customer's purchasing staff changed. Suddenly the janitorial service company lost the business—their largest customer. There was no time to react. In fact, the company was stuck with hundreds of thousands of dollars in inventory, products purchased to supply especially that customer. Another client was a clothing wholesaler who acquired a large customer. He went from doing business out of their garage to leasing a large distribution facility. Well, at some point that large customer went away, and he was stuck with an expensive lease and much more space than he needed. Of course, the owner had guaranteed the lease personally. These folks had a big hole to climb out of and, because of the personal guarantee, relatively few options.

If you have a large customer, obviously you don't want to give them up. What you do want to do, however, is use this business as the springboard to acquire other business. Your job is always to dilute the proportion of business that this large customer accounts for. Start today! Every day that you delay puts you closer to real danger.

24. Analyze the areas that you service. Determine why your strongest area is so strong and begin to duplicate that in your weaker areas. You should be able to determine what your market share is. Set a goal to increase share, and set an action plan to increase that share.

25. and 26. Let's look at some real truths about salespeople. First, they perform better when their compensation is based directly upon their sales. Just think about it. When you started your business (or when the founder started it), do you remember the adrenaline that flowed when you knew that if you didn't make the sale you might not have groceries at home? That adrenaline—and yes, maybe the fear—drove you to succeed. Salespeople react exactly the same way. Providing the correct motivation ensures that your sales staff will work at the top of their game. Part of your job will be to determine the basis for their compensation. If your salespeople have some control over the sales price and, as a result, can affect gross margin, then their compensation should be based upon margin. Conversely, if they have no control over the selling price, then pay them based upon sales.

The second truth is that no matter how much they may protest, your sales staff needs to be managed. They must provide you with weekly reports detailing who they visited, what the potential business is, and what the next step will be. They should also provide you with their planned schedule for the week and, on a monthly basis, give you their top twenty prospects for the upcoming month. It is your job to take that report and meet face-to-face with each salesperson. Give them lots of "attaboys," but at the same time challenge them. Ask specifically about sales that they did not close and find out what they could have done better to close the sale. Every lost sale should be an educational experience. You will find my Sales Management Process in chapter 14, "Pay Your Way to Recovery."

27. Intelligence regarding your competitors is important. Dig down deep and determine what it is that they really do well. Once you know your adversary, your chances of defeating them rise exponentially. Also, please

remember that your competitors are exactly that—your competitors, not your enemies. Use them to make you better and stronger, but don't focus on destroying them. I learned this the hard way early in my career. As CEO of a transportation company, I had a competitor who had been in the area longer than I had and was fairly well-entrenched politically. Additionally, he had a criminal background and did not always "play fair." Unfortunately for me, he also did a good job operating his company and generally proved to be a real thorn in my side. I absolutely forgot that he was not my enemy. I didn't give him a chance to make my company bigger and stronger. I just focused on destroying him. Most decisions that I made were directed at causing him pain rather than making my company more profitable. The end results really weren't good. Did he have some pain, and did I get some momentary feelings of satisfaction? You bet! Was I able to maximize my profitability and feel great about my company? Absolutely not! It was an expensive mistake and one that you should not duplicate.

28. Now take a deep breath and give some real thought to the state of your industry. What do you think the trends will be? If you believe that the future is bright and the industry is growing, then you must set out an action plan that describes exactly what you will do to take advantage of the positive industry outlook. If, on the other hand, you believe that the industry future is not as bright, you must do the same thing. Set out an action plan that describes what you will do to survive in this tough environment. Whatever the situation is, an action plan is mandatory.

29. It's time for more analysis on your part. Given your current facilities and personnel, how much more product can you manufacture, or how much more revenue can you generate? If you are not at least at 80 percent of your potential, you must create an action plan to enable you to maximize your production and revenue. If you are in manufacturing, can you streamline the manufacturing process by applying lean manufacturing processes? If you are in distribution, can you offer more effective motivating factors for your sales group? If you are at capacity, can you add additional shifts? What else can you do?

30. I had a manufacturing client who gave up significant profit because he would produce entire production runs and only then realize the product was defective in some way. Whatever type of manufacturing you are

engaged in should always incorporate a thorough examination of the first item produced in any run, as well as some sampling techniques as the run continues.

Another problem this manufacturing client encountered was significant machine downtime. His company was paying little attention to preventive maintenance. Once a preventative maintenance program was implemented, the problems vanished. Remember, the cheapest maintenance is the most proactive maintenance.

31. Entirely too many companies simply take the depreciation allowance and wait until replacing that equipment when it is in the "urgent and important" quadrant,[3] rather than being proactive and never letting the replacement get to the urgent range. Begin a sinking fund for anticipated replacement today. Additionally, making a decision to purchase capital equipment should never be based upon "gut" or your desire to have the latest and greatest. This is another case in which you can learn from my mistakes. While serving as CEO for the transportation company, I fell in love with the latest and greatest dispatching system. It cost over $600,000. I received quite a bit of publicity when I implemented it, and I was sure my "archenemy" competitor was experiencing heartburn as a result. The truth was it provided very little return on investment. I would have been much better served not to "fall in love." A thorough return on investment calculation should be done before any assets are acquired.

32. –34. Optimize your computer system. Are you getting all the reports mentioned in these questions, and on a timely basis? If not, it's time to find out why and to do whatever it takes so they are available for you and for your management. Use these reports first and foremost as a decision-making tool, and then for any historical value they may provide.

35. and 36. Well, based on the fact that you bought this book, you are either a masochist or you are having financial difficulties. Write down how much you currently owe and the maximum amount you can borrow. Be honest with yourself and write down the conditions that prevent you from having a greater borrowing capacity. Start taking actions that will allow you to increase your borrowing limits. One of the most effective steps that you can take is the development of both a long-term and a short-term cash

---

3 See Stephen R. Covey, *The 7 Habits of Highly Effective People* (Simon & Schuster, 1989). All four quadrants will be explained in more detail in chapter 7, "Lead Your Way to Recovery."

flow projection. You will have much more success saying to your loan officer, "Bob, I am going to have a cash shortfall in six weeks, and I'll need some financing to bridge that shortfall," rather than saying, "Bob, I'm out of money; how much can I borrow today?" See the difference?

37. This is a question that always draws a quick response. You've obviously thought about (perhaps dreamed about) what you would do if you had an additional $200,000 right now. Possibly you would pay off some of your company's debts. Perhaps you would take advantage of some quantity discounts your vendors are offering. Give this some real thought, and then create an action plan to develop those additional funds. The only wrong answer here would be, "I'd use that money to buy a plane ticket and go to some far-off island." This is escapism. If you really wanted to escape you would be buying travel books, not this book.

38. Leveraging your receivables or inventory may be a way to raise the money we discussed in the previous question. Interestingly, when I suggest the use of asset-based financing (or factoring, as it used to be called), the expression on my clients' faces usually looks like they have smelled something really, really awful. The mere mention of these words clearly conjures up bad visions. The truth is that sometimes asset-based financing is not only a good solution, it is the only solution. Utilizing this method means that you borrow money based on the amount of your good receivables and inventory. You usually get your maximum borrowing level approved in advance, and then you borrow based upon your needs. In most cases, lenders want the receivable collections to go directly to them. This is a resource that should not be overlooked, but it must be managed very carefully because it is quite expensive. Please note that asset-based financing is never intended to be a permanent solution. It is just to be used until a more traditional lender will take care of your borrowing needs. You must develop a plan to make the move to traditional borrowing.

39. How satisfied are you with your compensation? Compare your salary to a realistic estimate of what you could earn working for another company. Take into consideration all of the "perks" (like cars, etc.) when figuring out how much you earn, and don't forget to include proceeds from cash sales if you are not reporting them. (I am sure that is not the case.) My experience has been that business owners seem to operate at two extremes. They either don't pay themselves enough,

because they are not operating efficiently and need the money in other parts of the company, or they are taking so much out that the company is struggling to survive.

One of my client companies had three owners. The company produced about $5 million in revenue, and each owner was paid over $280,000. It will probably come as no surprise to you that the company was struggling. The surprise to me was that those owners were open to any type of change other than a reduction of their salaries. It made for a very difficult project.

Don't misunderstand me; I'm not suggesting that owners should not pay themselves the maximum amount that the company can tolerate, because that is exactly what I believe that they should do. There has to be a reward for all of the risk that you take as an owner. But the important thing to remember is that your real job is the creation of wealth for you and your family. And I don't mean the temporary kind of wealth that comes from a paycheck (even a good paycheck), but the much more permanent type of wealth that comes from owning a company that is producing significant profit and cash.

40. This is a good time to evaluate your employees and their earnings. How many employees do you have now, compared to the number you had a year ago? Divide your sales for this year by the number of employees to calculate the sales dollars per employee. Do the same for the previous year. Is the number going up or down? If the sales per employee are going down, this is a bad sign, and you must find the reason behind the decrease and deal with it. It is axiomatic that when sales per employee drops, so do profit levels.

41. Calculate the number of employees who have left your company for whatever reason over the past twelve months. Divide that number by your total employees. That gives you your turnover rate. If it is much higher than 5 percent, you may have a problem. Begin to calculate what your turnover costs the company. Include the cost of locating and hiring a new employee and the amount that it costs to train them. Add the cost of diminished productivity. A rule of thumb might be that the first six weeks of a new employee's tenure are truly nonproductive. If you multiply the total cost of a new employee by the number of employees that left your company, you will have the cost of your turnover.

42. If you don't have a pay-for-performance plan of some type for all of your employees, you are missing the boat. Employees who are rewarded based upon performance perform at a significantly higher level than employees who receive entitlements such as Christmas bonuses, or salary increases based only upon how long they have worked at a company or how much their supervisor likes them. Entitlements are fine as long as everything is good, but just try to cancel an entitlement like Christmas bonuses and see how long it takes for you to hear the words, "Where is my money?" You and I know the real truth. It's not their money. Employees paid on a performance basis have no one to ask about bonuses other than themselves. You will find out how to create an incentive plan in chapter 14, "Pay Your Way to Recovery."

43. If you have a pay-for-performance plan in effect, how effective is it? Can you calculate how much it has done for you? If not, you may well be using the wrong plan.

44. If your company is typical, inventory is a significant portion of your assets. How well are you managing that asset? You should know what the inventory turn is for every inventory item. Slow-turning items should be evaluated and a plan should be devised to reduce the quantity on hand. In reviewing the inventory turn for one of my clients, we noted that their overall inventory was turning three times per year, while the average turn for the industry was six. While examining the detail behind the inventory, we found numerous items had not moved for months or even years. A carefully developed plan allowed the company to dispose of a significant amount of these slow-moving items. Some of them were sold on eBay, and some were returned to vendors at a discount. In all, over $100,000 in cash was raised using this process. Odds are you have old inventory that can be converted to cash .If you will e-mail me at freestuff@profitabilitypartners.com, I will send you a spreadsheet with the formula for calculating inventory turn. You should always minimize your investment in inventory, because there are very real costs associated with excess inventory, including the cost of handling the material and possible additional inventory shortage.

45. It is important to protect that big investment you have in inventory. Wherever you keep inventory must be secure, and inventory must be withdrawn in a manner that, when removed, allows you to charge it

to cost of sales in a timely manner. If you don't know how much you have in inventory, how can you possibly know how much to purchase? Additionally, there is nothing more defeating than to believe that you are making a profit only to have it wiped out by a previously undisclosed inventory shortage. You can easily find inexpensive accounting software that can help you track the inventory. You may want to get some outside help to identify the right software for you.

46. This goes back to securing your inventory and having an appropriate withdrawal process. Some inventories have outstanding market value as resale items. Controls are vital.

47. and 48. You must know what your most profitable products are. It is not enough to take a guess; you must have incontrovertible, empirical data. This means that you must do an excellent job in allocating overhead expenses to each product line. There are several ways to allocate costs, ranging from projected sales to the cost of labor required to complete the product. Talk with your advisors as to which method is the right one for your company. It is also very important that you accurately track labor and material costs that go into each product line. Most of today's accounting software allows you to monitor these costs.

49. – 51. Now is the time for a little introspective thinking about your key employees. Set up a simple spreadsheet on which you list each of your key employees, along with their position, salary, and strengths and weaknesses. Also indicate whether you are satisfied with their performance. Looking coldly and clinically at their strengths and weaknesses, note whether you would hire them again, knowing what you know now. This is important. If you would not rehire them, they probably should not be working for you now. Rate each of these employees on a scale of 1 to 10. If you have any employees whom you have not rated at least at a 9 or 10, you must develop a plan to ensure that they can become a 9 or 10. Create a career development plan for each employee, regardless of his or her current position. If you hire good employees and invest in their development, you will yield great dividends. One of the most striking examples of this happened when I worked for a division of a large multidivision department store chain. We hired a young man as a janitor who recently had come over from Cuba. The company recognized the talent and work ethic he possessed and created a career path for him to follow. He retired

as president of one of the parent company's divisions. In the event that you determine you cannot continue their employment, we will have some additional information for you in chapter 14, "The People Side of the Business."

52. When we perform an analysis at a client company, one of the most common employee concerns is the lack of communication. Even if you do not hold staff meetings once a week, you probably don't feel a need for more communication. After all, you manage by walking around, don't you? You know what's going on. You even talked with Bob in Shipping about a month ago, didn't you? Or was it a year ago? The problem is that the rest of your team may not have that big picture knowledge, and believe me, it really concerns them.

You must have a well-organized staff meeting. Each meeting should have a specific agenda. The meeting should never last more than an hour, and a regular time and day must be established for the meeting. It must be held without regard to who is or who is not present. If you are not able to attend, you must appoint a substitute chairperson. During the course of the meeting, each key employee should report on where he or she stands with regard to their specific goals. If the employee is not on goal, what is being done to achieve the goal? This is one way you can move your company from an operation where every employee looks to you for all the answers to a company where every employee is empowered and has accepted full responsibility for their area of expertise. (And, of course, you have been only too happy to accept that responsibility, because you have all the answers, don't you?) A meeting cannot be deemed to be productive unless specific assignments are given out, on which a report is expected at the next meeting.

Remember, this is not a social affair. Keep it businesslike and non-threatening. Above all, watch the time. Don't let it become a marathon session. One of my clients removed all of the chairs in the meeting room, because he found that people tended to get to the point quicker if they were standing instead of sitting comfortably. You will find a process for holding effective staff meetings in chapter 9, "The Harder I Work."

53. In his book *The 7 Habits of Highly Effective People,* Dr. Stephen R. Covey defines an *urgent* problem as a problem that, if left unresolved, will cause really bad things to happen. An example of an urgent problem is a

continuing cash deficit that has gone unchecked and has resulted in an overdrawn bank account and a payroll that cannot be met. Write down your most urgent problem. (Yes, you have at least one urgent problem, or you would not be reading this book.) Create an action plan to resolve this problem. Example: If you have an overdrawn bank account, resolve to find enough money to bring it back into the black. Use whatever methods necessary. Talk to your banker or an asset-based lender. Talk to friends and relatives. Do what it takes.

54. Dr. Covey defines an *important* problem as a problem that, if left unresolved, will become an urgent problem. An example of an important problem would be if you had a short-term cash flow plan and had found that in six weeks you would encounter a cash shortfall. You would now have time to explore alternative solutions to this issue. Define your most important problem. Yes, you have at least one of them also. Again, create an action plan to keep this problem from becoming urgent.

55. Yes, this sounds weird. But it is very important. Just think, you have no limitations, nothing to stand in your way from keeping your company from changing any way that you like. Once you wave the wand, your company has changed completely, with no other effort on your part. Now, once you have decided what you would like it to look like, create an action plan to begin to move it in that direction. Establish due dates for each of the goals. Be sure that you stay on plan and begin the process of change.

CHAPTER 6

The Lab Work

N ow that we have a complete health history and physical examination, we need to run some lab tests. Just as the doctor's lab analyzes your various specimens and provides results that allow the doctor to chart a plan of action for you, so will this lab work assist you in developing a plan of action.

I have never met a business owner who has a real sense of what his company should earn. Yes, a business owner may have some vague idea of what they would like to earn, but it is usually not based upon any type of empirical evidence. In this section, we will find out what companies of your size and in your industry actually earn, and as a result of that knowledge, determine how much profit you are leaving on the table.

We want to measure ourselves against two important standards. The first is our own Best Established Performance. If you lay out your operating results (broken down into some broad categories such as revenue, gross margin, operating expenses excluding depreciation and amortization, depreciation and amortization, other income and expenses, and pretax profit), you will likely find that you never achieve your best results in each category within the same year. Best Established Performance shows you what your profit could be if you were to achieve your best results in each of the above-mentioned categories at the same time. This is important information for you, because it only challenges you to reach performance levels that you have already reached, although it will challenge you to reach those levels all within the same year.

The second standard against which to measure yourself is the level of performance attained by the upper quartile of companies in your industry. Several sources offer comparative financial data for companies in your industry. One such company is Risk Management Association (800-677-7621, or www.rmahq.org). You can find others through an Internet search, and they are all fairly pricey. I can also provide you with the comparative data at a substantial savings. You can order your comparative financial data by e-mailing me your contact phone number at sandy@profitabilitypartners.com. We can talk so that I can fully understand exactly what business you are in and I can be sure you get the correct comparatives.

But even with the right comparative data, how are you going to get this important comparison done? Don't worry. You've bought the book, and if you will e-mail me at freestuff@profitabilitypartners.com, I will send you a spreadsheet that will allow you to enter your own data and find out how much you are leaving on the table. On the following pages, you will see what the spreadsheet and the results look like. You will find the data entry instructions after the spreadsheet.

XYZ Company, Inc.
Financial Analysis Data Entry Sheet
Five years ending 12/31/03

Assets		1999		2000		2001		2002		2003	BEP
Cash	$	1,037	$	17,385	$	10,780	$	1,852	$	4,471	
Accts. Rec.-Net	$	1,221,628	$	883,667	$	957,838	$	1,050,379	$	810,681	
Quick Assets	$	1,222,665	$	901,052	$	968,618	$	1,052,231	$	815,152	
Inventory	$	71,043	$	85,487	$	112,299	$	113,052	$	179,538	
Other Current Assets	$	170,191	$	38,006	$	-	$	-	$	-	
Total Current Assets	$	1,463,899	$	1,024,545	$	1,080,917	$	1,165,283	$	994,690	
Net Property and Equip	$	325,806	$	399,239	$	495,272	$	234,536	$	106,459	
Other Assets	$	-	$	-	$	-	$	-	$	12,215	
Total Assets	$	1,789,705	$	1,423,784	$	1,576,189	$	1,399,819	$	1,113,364	
Liabilities & Shareholders Equity											
Current Liabilities	$	1,085,216	$	807,481	$	920,119	$	1,359,179	$	1,005,691	
Long Term Debt	$	223,253	$	260,465	$	374,655	$	178,025	$	212,466	
Other Liabilities	$	-	$	-	$	-	$	-	$	-	
Shareholders' Equity	$	481,236	$	355,838	$	281,415	$	(137,385)	$	(104,793)	
Total Liabilities and Shareholders' Equity	$	1,789,705	$	1,423,784	$	1,576,189	$	1,399,819	$	1,113,364	

Figure 6.1a. Sample Financial Analysis Data Entry Sheets

Ratio Analysis

Down = Negative Trend; Up = Positive Trend; Flat = Change less than 5% +/-

	1999	2000	2001	2002	2003	mean	Upper Quart	delta
Liquidity								
Quick Ratio	1.13	1.12	1.05	0.77	0.81	0.98	2.10	-16.95%
Current Ratio	1.35	1.27	1.17	0.86	0.99	1.13	2.50	-12.30%
Activity								
Inventory Turnover	63.33	42.34	27.90	33.29	15.48	36.47		-57.55%
Fixed Asset Turnover	17.76	12.10	9.09	21.07	38.39	19.68	43.60	95.07%
Total Asset Turnover	3.23	3.39	2.85	3.53	3.67	3.34	3.90	10.03%
Days Sales Outstanding	77.05	66.79	77.69	77.58	72.40	74.30	38.00	-2.57%
Leverage								
Funded Debt/Equity Ratio	0.46	0.73	1.33	(1.30)	(2.03)	(0.16)		1173.42%
Current Liabilities/equity Ratio	2.26	2.27	3.27	(9.89)	(9.60)	(2.34)		310.26%
Total Debt/Equity Ratio	2.72	3.00	4.60	(11.19)	(11.62)	(2.50)	0.70	365.26%
Interest Coverage	2.50	0.35	0.12	(2.95)	1.61	0.33	12.00	396.53%
Profitability								
Gross Margin	22.25%	25.04%	30.37%	23.84%	31.99%	26.70%	38.90%	19.83%
Operating Margin	4.60%	2.76%	3.63%	-1.41%	5.83%	3.08%	12.60%	89.19%
Profit Margin	1.75%	-1.97%	-1.15%	-6.46%	0.80%	-1.41%	12.30%	-156.69%
EBITDA	$ 247,193	$ 133,415	$ 110,416	$ (119,773)	$ 188,277	111,905		68.25%
EBITDA Percentage	4.27%	2.76%	2.45%	-2.42%	4.61%	2%		97.35%
Return to Invested Capital	$ 169,113	$ 50,824	$ 6,801	$ (238,471)	$ 85,671	14,787		479.35%
FYE Invested Capital	$ 704,489	$ 616,303	656,070	40,640	107,673	425,035		-74.67%
Return on Invested Capital %	24.01%	8.25%	1.04%	-586.79%	79.57%	-94.8%		-183.94%
Return on Shareholders' Equity	21.09%	-26.78%	-18.43%	232.34%	-31.10%	35.4%	35.00%	-187.80%

Figure 6.1b. Sample Financial Analysis Data Entry Sheets

Statement of Operations and Retained Earnings

	1999	2000	2001	2002	2,003	BDP	Upper Quartile
Revenues	$ 5,787,292	$ 4,828,935	$ 4,499,889	$ 4,941,786	$ 4,087,221	$ 5,787,292	$ 5,787,292
Cost of Goods Sold	$ 4,499,429	$ 3,619,883	$ 3,133,238	$ 3,763,758	$ 2,779,595	$ 3,935,937	$ 3,935,937
Gross Margin	$ 1,287,863	$ 1,209,052	$ 1,366,651	$ 1,178,028	$ 1,307,626	$ 1,851,355	$ 1,851,355
Gross Margin Percent	22.25%	25.04%	30.37%	23.84%	31.99%	31.99%	31.99%
Operating Expenses Excluding							
Depreciation	$ 943,695	$ 993,110	$ 1,099,727	$ 1,128,971	$ 966,695	$ 943,329	$ 1,250,634
%	16.3%	20.6%	24.4%	22.8%	23.7%	16.30%	
Depreciation & Amortization	$ 78,080	$ 82,591	$ 103,615	$ 118,698	$ 102,606	$ 97,118	$ 57,873 m
Operating Expenses	$ 1,021,775	$ 1,075,701	$ 1,203,342	$ 1,247,669	$ 1,069,301	$ 1,040,447	$ 1,308,507
Operating Income	$ 266,088	$ 133,351	$ 163,309	$ (69,641)	$ 238,325	$ 810,908	$ 542,848
Operating Income Percent	4.60%	2.76%	3.63%	-1.41%	5.83%	14.01%	9.38%
Other (Income) and Expense							
Interest	$ 67,601	$ 146,108	$ 58,664	$ 80,725	$ 53,077	$ 81,235	$ 63,081 m
Officers Salary	$ 104,488	$ 103,610	$ 168,265	$ 168,830	$ 152,654	$ 139,569	$ 150,470 m
Other - net	$ (7,513)	$ (21,083)	$ (11,757)	$ -	$ -	$ (8,071)	$ 17,362 m
Total Other (Income) and Expense	$ 164,576	$ 228,635	$ 215,172	$ 249,555	$ 205,731	$ 212,734	$ 230,913
Net Income	$ 101,512	$ (95,284)	$ (51,863)	$ (319,196)	$ 32,594	$ 598,174	$ 311,935
Profit Margin	1.75%	-1.97%	-1.15%	-6.46%	0.80%	10.34%	5.39%
Retained Earnings - Beginning	$ 382,164	$ 471,776	$ 346,378	$ 271,954	$ (146,846)	$ (146,846)	
Income Taxes	$ -	$ -	$ -	$ -	$ -	$ -	
Adjustments	$ (11,900)	$ (30,114)	$ (22,560)	$ (99,604)	$ (114,252)		
Retained Earnings - Ending	$ 471,776	$ 346,378	$ 271,954	$ (146,846)	451,329		

Figure 6.2. Statement of Operations and Retained Earnings

XYZ Company, Inc.
Balance Sheet

	FY 1999	FY2000	FY 2001	FY 2002	FY 2003
Assets					
Cash	$ 1,037	$ 17,385	$ 10,780	$ 1,852	$ 4,471
Accounts Receivable - Net	$ 1,221,628	$ 883,667	$ 957,838	$ 1,050,379	$ 810,681
Quick Assets	$ 1,222,665	$ 901,052	$ 968,618	$ 1,052,231	$ 815,152
Inventory	$ 71,043	$ 85,487	$ 112,299	$ 113,052	$ 179,538
Other Current Assets	$ 170,191	$ 38,006	$ -	$ -	$ -
Total Current Assets	$ 1,463,899	$ 1,024,545	$ 1,080,917	$ 1,165,283	$ 994,690
Net Property and Equipment	$ 325,806	$ 399,239	$ 495,272	$ 234,536	$ 106,459
Other Assets	$ -	$ -	$ -	$ -	$ 12,215
Total Assets	$ 1,789,705	$ 1,423,784	$ 1,576,189	$ 1,399,819	$ 1,113,364
Liabilities and Shareholders' Equity					
Current Liabilities	$ 1,085,216	$ 807,481	$ 920,119	$ 1,359,179	$ 1,005,691
Long Term Debt	$ 223,253	$ 260,465	$ 374,655	$ 178,025	$ 212,466
Other Liabilities	$ -	$ -	$ -	$ -	$ -
Shareholders' Equity	$ 481,236	$ 355,838	$ 281,415	$ (137,385)	$ (104,793)
Total Liabilities and Shareholders' Equity	$ 1,789,705	$ 1,423,784	$ 1,576,189	$ 1,399,819	$ 1,113,364

Figure 6.3 Sample Five-Year Balance Sheet

XYZ Company, Inc.
For the Periods Ending 1999 through 2003
Income Statement

	1999	2000	2001	2002	2003	Upper Quart.	BEP
Revenues	$ 5,787,292	$ 4,828,935	$ 4,499,889	$ 4,941,786	$ 4,087,221	$ 5,787,292	$ 5,787,292
Cost of Goods Sold	$ 4,499,429	$ 3,619,883	$ 3,133,238	$ 3,763,758	$ 2,779,595	$ 3,935,937	$ 3,935,937
Gross Margin	$ 1,287,863	$ 1,209,052	$ 1,366,651	$ 1,178,028	$ 1,307,626	$ 1,851,355	$ 1,851,355
Gross Margin Percent	22.3%	25.0%	30.4%	23.8%	32.0%	31.99%	32.0%
Operating Expenses Excluding Depreciation	$ 943,695	$ 993,110	$ 1,099,727	$ 1,128,971	$ 966,695	$ 1,250,634	$ 943,329
Depreciation & Amortization	$ 78,080	$ 82,591	$ 103,615	$ 118,698	$ 102,606		$ 97,118
Operating Expenses	$ 1,021,775	$ 1,075,701	$ 1,203,342	$ 1,247,669	$ 1,069,301	$ 1,308,507	$ 1,040,447
Operating Income	$ 266,088	$ 133,351	$ 163,309	$ (69,641)	$ 238,325	$ 542,848	$ 810,908
Operating Income Percent	4.6%	2.8%	3.6%	-1.4%	5.8%	9.4%	14.0%
Other (Income) and Expense	$	$	$	$	$	$	$
Interest	67,601	146,108	58,664	80,725	53,077	63,081	81,235
Officers Salary	104,488	103,610	168,265	168,830	152,654	150,470	139,569
Other - Net	(7,513)	(21,083)	(11,757)	-	-	17,362	(8,071)
Total Other (Income) and Expense	$ 164,576	$ 228,635	$ 215,172	$ 249,555	$ 205,731	$ 230,913	$ 212,734
Net Income	$ 101,512	$ (95,284)	$ (51,863)	$ (319,196)	$ 32,594	$ 311,935	$ 598,174
Profit Margin	1.8%	-2.0%	-1.2%	-6.5%	0.8%	5.4%	10.3%
Retained Earnings - Beginning	$ 382,164	$ 471,776	$ 346,378	$ 271,954	$ (146,846)	$	$ (146,846)
Prior Period Adjustment	$ -	$ -	$ -	$ -	$ -	$	$ -
Sub S Distributions	$ (11,900)	$ (30,114)	$ (22,560)	$ (99,604)	$ (114,252)	$	$ -
Retained Earnings - Ending	$ 471,776	$ 346,378	$ 271,954	$ (146,846)		$	$ 451,329

Figure 6.4. Sample Five-Year Income Statement

XYZ Company, Inc.
For the Periods Ending 1999 through 2003
Selected Ratios

RATIO ANALYSIS	1999	2000	2001	2002	2003	MEAN	UPPER Q	DELTA
Down = Negative trend; Up = Positive trend; Flat = Change less than +/-5%								
Liquidity								
Quick Ratio	1.13	1.12	1.05	0.77	0.81	0.98	2.10	-16.95%
Current Ratio	1.35	1.27	1.17	0.86	0.99	1.13	2.50	-12.30%
Activity								
Inventory Turnover	63.33	42.34	27.90	33.29	15.48	36.47	0.00	-57.55%
Fixed Asset Turnover	17.76	12.10	9.09	21.07	38.39	19.68	43.60	95.07%
Total Asset Turnover	3.23	3.39	2.85	3.53	3.67	3.34	3.90	10.03%
Days Sales Outstanding	77.05	66.79	77.69	77.58	72.40	74.30	38.00	-2.57%
							0.00	
							0.00	
Leverage								
Funded Debt/Equity Ratio	0.46	0.73	1.33	(1.30)	(2.03)	(0.16)	0.00	1173.42%
Current Liabilities/Equity Ratio	2.26	2.27	3.27	(9.89)	(9.60)	(2.34)	0.00	310.26%
Total Debt/Equity Ratio	2.72	3.00	4.60	(11.19)	(11.62)	(2.50)	0.70	365.26%
Interest Coverage	2.50	0.35	0.12	(2.95)	1.61	0.33	12.00	396.53%
							0.00	
							0.00	
Profitability								
Gross Margin	22.3%	25.0%	30.4%	23.8%	32.0%	26.7%	38.9%	19.83%
Operating Margin	4.6%	2.8%	3.6%	-1.4%	5.8%	3.1%	12.6%	89.19%
Profit Margin	1.8%	-2.0%	-1.2%	-6.5%	0.8%	-1.4%	12.3%	-156.69%
EBITDA	247,192.84	133,414.79	110,415.76	(119,773.23)	188,276.76	111,905.38	0.0%	68.25%
EBITDA Percentage	4.27%	2.76%	2.45%	-2.42%	4.61%	2.33%	0.0%	97.35%
Return to Invested Capital	169,112.84	50,823.79	6,800.76	(238,471.23)	85,670.76	14,787.38	0.0%	479.35%
FYE Invested Capital	704,489	616,303	656,070	40,640	107,673	425,035	0.0%	-74.67%
Return on Invested Capital Percentage	24.0%	8.2%	1.0%	-586.8%	79.6%	-94.8%	0.0%	-183.94%
Return on Shareholders' Equity	21.1%	-26.8%	-18.4%	232.3%	-31.1%	35.4%	35.0%	-187.80%

Figure 6.5. Sample Five-Year Selected Ratios

Data Entry Instructions for Financial Analysis Data Entry Sheets

Collect and have in front of you the financial statements from the past five years. Then follow the instructions for each of the rows listed below:

Years. Place the year that you are using for comparison in each of the designated five columns.

Cash. From your balance sheets, enter the end-of-the-year cash balance for each of the five comparative years.

Accounts Receivable. From your balance sheets, enter the end-of-the-year accounts receivable balance for each of the five comparative years.

Quick Assets. Enter nothing. The spreadsheet will calculate this number.

Inventory. From your balance sheets, enter the end-of-the-year inventory balance for each of the five comparative years.

Other Current Assets. From your balance sheets, enter the end-of-the-year balance for all of the other current assets for each of the five comparative years.

Total Current Assets. Enter nothing. The spreadsheet will calculate this number.

Net Property & Equipment. From your balance sheets, enter your total fixed assets reduced by your accumulated depreciation for each of the five comparative years.

Other Assets. From your balance sheets, enter all of the other assets for each of the five comparative years.

Total Assets. Enter nothing. The spreadsheet will calculate this number.

Current Liabilities. From your balance sheets, enter the current liabilities for each of the five comparative years.

Long-Term Liabilities. From your balance sheets, enter the long-term liabilities for each of the five years.

Other Liabilities. From your balance sheets, enter all liabilities not previously entered for each of the five years.

Shareholder's Equity. From your balance sheets, enter the total shareholder's equity, including retained earnings and capital stock.

Total Liabilities and Shareholder's Equity. Enter nothing. The spreadsheet will calculate this number. Please note that the total assets must equal the Total Liabilities and Shareholder's Equity. If they are not equal, go back and review your entries.

Revenues. From your income statement, enter the total revenues for each of the five years.

Cost of Goods Sold. From your income statement, enter the total cost of goods sold for each of the five years.

Gross Margin. Enter nothing. The spreadsheet will compute the gross margin.

Gross Margin Percent. Enter nothing. The spreadsheet will compute the gross margin percentage.

Operating Expenses Excluding Depreciation. From your income statement enter your operating expenses without depreciation, interest, officer's salary and net other expense for each of the five years. .

Depreciation. From your income statement, enter the depreciation expense for each of the five years.

Total Operating Expenses. Enter nothing. The spreadsheet will compute the total operating expenses.

Interest Expense. From your income statements, enter the interest expense for each of the five years.

Officer's Salary. From your income statement, enter the officer's salary for each of the five years.

Other—Net. From your income statement, enter the net other expense for each of the five years.

Total Other Income and Expense. Enter nothing. The spreadsheet will compute this amount.

Net Income. Enter nothing. The spreadsheet will compute this amount.

Profit Margin. Enter nothing. The spreadsheet will calculate this percentage.

Retained Earnings—Beginning. For the first year, enter your retained earnings from your balance sheet. For the remaining years, enter nothing, as the beginning balance will be calculated by the spreadsheet.

Income Taxes. From your income statement, enter your income tax amount for each of the five years.

Adjustments. From your balance sheets, enter any adjustments to retained earnings for each of the five years.

Retained Earnings—Ending. Enter nothing. The spreadsheet will compute this amount. Be sure that the calculated amount equals the retained earnings on your balance sheets.

Ratios. Enter nothing in any of the five years. The spreadsheet will compute the ratios.

Best Established Performance Column

Revenue. Enter the highest of the five years in this column. Also enter that number in the Upper Quartile column.

Cost of Goods Sold. Enter nothing. This number will be computed automatically.

Gross Margin. Enter nothing. This number will be computed automatically.

Gross Margin Percent. Enter the highest gross margin percentage of the five years in this cell.

Operating Expenses Excluding Depreciation. Enter nothing. The spreadsheet will compute this cell.

Operating Expenses Excluding Depreciation %. Enter the lowest percentage of the five years in this cell.

Depreciation. Enter nothing. This number will be computed automatically.

Operating Expenses. Enter nothing. This number will be computed automatically.

Operating Income. Enter nothing. This number will be computed automatically.

Interest. Enter nothing. This number will be computed automatically.

Officer's Salary. Enter nothing. This number will be computed automatically.

Other—Net. Enter nothing. This number will be computed automatically.

Net Income. Enter nothing. This number will be computed automatically.

Profit Margin. Enter nothing. This number will be computed automatically.

Upper Quartile

Revenues. Enter the revenue from the Best Established Performance column.

Cost of Goods Sold. Enter nothing. This number will be automatically computed.

Gross Margin. Enter nothing. This number will be automatically computed.

Gross Margin Percent. Enter the gross margin percentage from the upper quartile data. If upper quartile gross margin is not available, multiply the average industry gross margin percentage and multiply that by 1.20. Our experience is that the upper quartile companies are generally 20 percent better in this category.

Operating Expenses Excluding Depreciation. Enter nothing. This number will be automatically computed.

Depreciation. Enter the upper quartile percentage from your industry data.

Operating Expenses. Enter the upper quartile percentage from your industry's data. If the upper quartile gross margin is not available, reduce the industry average by 10 percent.

Interest. Enter the upper quartile percentage from your industry data.

Officer's Salary. Enter the upper quartile percentage from your industry data.

Other. Enter the upper quartile percentage from your industry data.

Net Income. Enter nothing. This number will be automatically computed.

Ratio Analysis

Actual ratios for the comparative years. Enter nothing. These numbers will be automatically computed.

Upper Quartile. Enter any of the upper quartile ratios that are available from your database.

So What Do All Those Numbers Mean?

Okay, now you have completed the financial analysis. Because you have completed the Financial Data Entry Sheet, you will notice that you have tabs titled BALSHT, INCMST, and RATIOS. If you will open those sheets, you will find that, because you have worked so hard entering the data, you have been rewarded with some powerful information. You are now going to review the fruits of your efforts to isolate the areas that present some great opportunities for improvement. You will find that the balance sheet will show you some interesting trends; it is used primarily as a basis for ratio analysis. The income statement will present some visible opportunities. You will note from the example in this book (which came from a real project) that the company had its best sales year in 1999, but it had its best gross margin performance in 2003, which was the most current year.

So based on this example, what do we know? We know that to achieve a very admirable gross margin percent increase, the company suffered a sales decrease of nearly 30 percent. That told us that the company's sales staff had not learned to sell value as opposed to selling price, which obviously was significantly easier in their high sales year. The solution in this case was to change the way that the sales staff was compensated, so that much of their pay was based upon what they sold.

Previously they were relatively unmotivated, as very little of their compensation was based on sales and margin. We also recognized that they did not really have a sales process that worked. After changing the compensation plan and teaching the sales staff a new sales process, the situation changed for the better. And, of course, we taught the owners how to manage the sales staff. We will discuss that process later in this book.

Returning to the income statement example, you will notice that the company's best net income was $101,512 in 1999, with two years of large losses. But you will also see that if they had achieved the best performance in each of the financial areas that they would have earned nearly $600,000, which is even better than what the upper quartile produced. What this really tells us is that the company was capable of earning significantly more than they did and that quick action had to be taken. (And it was.) The fact that the upper quartile also earned significantly more than the company did simply confirmed that there was real opportunity for improvement.

So we know that this company has severe sales problems, potentially fatal if left unattended. But, as they say in infomercials, "There's more!" If we look at the ratios, we find that the Days Sales Outstanding has continually run in the range of 70 days or more, while the upper quartile is only 38 days. This means that accounts receivable are way too high, which results in cash being much lower than it should be.

Think about it. This company is really experiencing the worst of all worlds. It is underperforming in the sales arena, and it is doing a very poor job of collecting the cash due on sales it does make. How do you think this business owner was sleeping? Can we all say together, "I'm a little low on cash, and I can't pay you?"

Of course, fortunately for that owner, there was a process to correct the poor collections, and we did correct it. We will discuss that process later in this book.

Explanation of Ratios

For your reference, here is a list of the various ratios you developed in your ratio analysis and their definitions:

Quick Ratio. Measures the ability of the firm to meet its obligations under distress conditions. At a minimum, the quick ratio should be 1 or higher, depending upon the industry.

Current Ratio. Measures the ability of the firm to meet its short-term obligations. Generally, the current ratio should be at least 2 to 1, so as to insulate the firm from unforeseen downturns in sales.

Inventory Turnover. Measures the efficiency of inventory control and purchasing. A low or declining turnover indicates that the firm's inventories are not being properly managed.

Fixed Asset Turnover. Measures the amount of investment in fixed assets that is generating a given level of sales. Relative to the industry, low ratios indicate poor sales management and underutilized assets.

Total Asset Turnover. Measures the amount of total investment that is generating a given level of sales. Relative to the industry, low ratios indicate poor sales management and underutilized assets.

Days Sales Outstanding. Measures how long a company's customers actually take to pay. How does it compare to the firm's stated policy and the industry average? A high collection period squeezes cash flow and constrains opportunities for expansion or causes additional borrowing.

Current Liabilities to Equity. Compares how much of the firm's assets are owned by its short-term creditors vs. equity holders. High or increasing ratios indicate that the firm is funding itself with debt instead of profits.

Funded Debt to Equity. Compares how much of the firm's assets are owned by its long-term creditors vs. equity holders. High or increasing ratios indicate that the firm is funding itself with debt instead of profits.

Total Debt to Equity. Compares how much of the firm's assets are owned by its creditors versus equity holders. Ratios above 60 percent indicate that the firm is funding itself with debt instead of profits.

Interest Coverage. This ratio is a measure of a firm's ability to meet interest payments. A high ratio may indicate that a borrower would have little difficulty in meeting the interest obligations of a loan. This ratio also serves as an indicator of a firm's capacity to take on additional debt.

Return on Equity. Measures the efficiency with which a firm employs its equity. At a minimum, the ROE should be greater than the Treasury bill rate, since the owners could earn this return with no risk or effort.

CHAPTER 7

Lead Your Way to Recovery

One of the things that you must do if your company is going to recover (no, let's make that "be vibrantly healthy") is to decide to turn your company into what I call an Enterprise of Excellence. Ken Blanchard has produced a great body of work in this area, particularly his book *Leading at a Higher Level.* Because of obvious time and space limitations, we are going to briefly discuss this concept here. My hope is that this discussion will not only help you improve your company, but it will also whet your appetite for more information on this vital subject. To learn more—much more!—you can find *Leading at a Higher Level* at www.kenblanchard.com.

Why Should I Want My Company to Be an Enterprise of Excellence?

Joe Paterno said, "You have to perform at a consistently higher level than others. That's the mark of a true professional." He also described the alternative: "You need to play with supreme confidence or else you'll lose again and losing becomes

people well informed, and let them use their brains, you'll be amazed how they can help manage costs and improve profitability. Of course, you also want to share your excess profits with them through a well-constructed pay-for-performance plan, such as the one we will discuss in chapter 14, "Pay Your Way to Recovery."

Just imagine what your company would look like if it achieved the trifecta. It should make you want to do whatever is necessary to get yourself into that rarified atmosphere.

Characteristics of an Enterprise of Excellence

- **The company pursues a driving vision.** A driving vision answers the questions, "Why are we here? And what should we be doing?" When everyone from the person sweeping the floor to the person at the very top of the corporate ladder buys into the vision, which includes a purpose, a description of what the future looks like, and specific values, the entire company has a focus that drives the desired business results toward a greater good. People truly live the vision. Everyone is aligned and marching in the same direction.

- **The company has a supreme focus on customer satisfaction.** Enterprises of Excellence know intimately who their customer is and measure the results accordingly. In fact, they are obsessive about the results. They focus on those results from the viewpoint of the customer.

- **The company empowers its employees by sharing power and information.** This is a real paradigm shift from the old style of organization, in which the owner jealously guarded all information and made it available to the employees only on a need-to-know basis. In Enterprises of Excellence, we see none of the "I am the boss and you are the drone" mentality that stifles creativity. Instead, employees are offered opportunities to become all they can be and help the organization thrive as effectively as they can. Also, making company information easily available builds trust and drives people to act like owners. Information is power. When employers and employees come together and create real synergy, everyone wins. When people feel they can contribute, their performance will always be better than when they do not.

If we want to become an Enterprise of Excellence, then leadership is how we get there. Leadership in Enterprises of Excellence operates significantly differently than leadership found in other organizations. Enterprises of Excellence don't have to rely on a great charismatic leader, but instead they rely on building a vision-driven organization that continues beyond the leader. The more you think about that statement, the more sense it makes. If you suddenly disappeared from the scene, wouldn't you want to know that your company would go on—and go on successfully? In this model, the role of leadership shifts from privileged status and power for its own sake (the Grand Poobah, if you will) toward a much more involved, long-term process. Once you have created the vision, as a leader your job is now to morph into a *servant* leader.

I recommend that you ask your key employees to rate the company on the characteristics that we just discussed. If your rating is low, don't be discouraged; rather be motivated and driven to dramatically improve the score the next time you ask for rating. Here is the form for you to use.

Enterprise of Excellence Survey

Remember, an Enterprise of Excellence is the most-wanted vendor, the most-wanted employer, and the most-wanted property. Please complete the survey below to determine how your company rates.

On a scale of 1 to 7, to what extent do you disagree or agree with the following statements? Here are the possible responses:

    1 = strongly disagree

    2 = disagree

    3 = slightly disagree

    4 = neutral

    5 = slightly agree

    6 = agree

    7 = strongly agree

Indicate your level of agreement or disagreement by placing the number that signifies your view of your organization in the blank next to each of the following statements.

Shared Information and Open Communication

_____ Needed information is readily available.

The Driving Vision

_____ We know why we are here and what we should be doing.

_____ Everyone in our organization is marching in the same direction.

Relentless Focus on Customer Results

_____ Everyone in our organization is totally committed to achieving the highest standards of quality and service.

_____ All of our systems have been created to make it easier for our customers to do business with us.

Sharing of Power

_____ People are able to have an impact on decisions that affect them.

Leadership

_____ Leaders know that leading is about serving rather than being served. There is no Grand Poobah.

Again, if you didn't score sixes and sevens, just make your mind up that you will take steps, using the strategy of change that we discussed earlier in this book, to get those sixes and sevens sooner rather than later. It all starts with creating a compelling vision.

Pursuing a Driving Vision

The biggest impediment blocking most managers from being great leaders is that there is no clear vision for the organization. It is important for leaders first to have a clear vision, because you only need leadership if you're going somewhere. If you and your people don't know where you are going, your leadership doesn't matter. My experience has been that only a very small percentage of companies I have worked with had employees who really understood the corporate vision. Without a well-communicated vision, people become lost in the minutia that makes up their day. There is an abundance of motion, but it is motion that makes up the whirlwind we discussed earlier. This certainly does not support the trifecta.

Once people have a vision of what the end game is, their ability to make great choices increases drastically. As each goal is achieved, the next needed action becomes obvious. Great vision helps us to be proactive. Peter Drucker said "The best way to predict your future is to create it." What an elegant thought! Create your future!

Creating an Effective Vision Statement

The litmus test for an effective vision statement is whether it can be used in making daily decisions. If it is not effective, it is just a useless piece of paper framed on the owner's desk or hanging on the wall. Let me give you an example of an ineffective vision. In the opening interview of a project, I asked the owner if he had a corporate vision, to which he proudly answered, "Yes. It is to be the best that we can be." I told him that was an interesting statement, but I just didn't understand how that helped anyone make their daily decisions. He had to agree with me that he had an ineffective vision statement.

So how do you create an effective vision statement? In his book *Leading at a Higher Level* (FT Press, 2009), Ken Blanchard tells us that a compelling vision has three key elements:

1. A major objective: What business are you really in?
2. A clear view of what lies ahead: What will your company look like when you succeed?
3. Well-defined principles: What guides your conduct and choices as you go through each day?

A major objective. The major objective is your company's real reason for being. It answers the question *why* you do what you do, rather than just explaining *what* it is that you do. It makes clear, from your customer's viewpoint, what business you are really in. Walt Disney had a great view of his major objective when he started his business. He said, "It is to make people happy." Isn't that very different from saying, "We are in the theme park business"? How would that drive the daily decisions people make about their conduct? Understanding the major objective drives everything the cast members (employees) do with their guests (customers).

Give Kids the World is an organization that raises money for children with terminal illnesses to realize their dreams of visiting Disney World, Sea World, or one of the other Orlando attractions. Their major objective is not "We take sick children on their dream trips," but "We make memories." Similarly, Microsoft's major objective is "to have a personal computer in every home running Microsoft software." Their potential customer is really every computer owner in the world. Having a clear major objective releases power that I am certain will amaze you.

A clear view of what lies ahead. A compelling vision cannot be theoretical. It should be a mental image you can actually see. Walt Disney's vision was expressed in the charge he gave every cast member: "Keep the same smile on people's faces when they leave the park as when they entered." At Give the Kids the World, they envision their kids, even in the last week of their lives, still laughing and talking to their families about their time in Orlando. And at Microsoft, they see their software running in every home in the world.

Well-defined principles. Principles define the way employees act on a day to day basis while doing their work. Principles answer the questions "By what rules do I want to conduct my life?" and" How do I want to conduct my life?" Values are beliefs you feel strongly about because you choose them over other alternatives. Values need to be consistently acted upon or they are only good intentions. They need to echo the principles of the employees of the company so that employees truly choose to live by them.

Most organizations with values either have too many of them or have not rank-ordered them. According to Ken Blanchard, research shows people cannot focus on more than three or four values that really impact behavior, and those values must be rank-ordered to be effective. Why? Because life is about value conflicts, and when these conflicts arise, people need to know which value to focus on.

A perfect example of the need for clearly ranking principles, or values, can be seen at Disney. The Disney theme parks have four rank-ordered values: safety, courtesy, the show, and efficiency. Why is safety the highest ranked value? Disney knew if guests were carried out of one of his parks on a stretcher, they would not have the same smiles on their faces leaving the park as they had when they entered.

The second-ranked value, courtesy, is demonstrated in the friendly attitude you expect at a Disney park. What if one of the cast members is answering a guest's question in a friendly, courteous manner, and he hears a scream that's not coming from a terrifying gravity-defying ride? If that cast member wants to act according to the park's rank-ordered values, he will excuse himself as quickly and politely as possible and race toward the scream. Why? Because the number-one value just called. If the values were not prioritized and the cast member was enjoying his conversation with the guest, he might point in the direction of the scream and say, "There is always someone screaming around here." If someone were to say to him later, "You were the closest to the scream; why didn't you do something?" his response could be, "I was dealing with our courtesy value." Life is a series of value conflicts, and you can't always act on two values at the same time.

Living Your Vision

Remember, once you create the vision, you can't just tack it to a wall and forget it. You have to talk about it and reinforce it constantly, or it will atrophy like a little-used muscle.

Your first task, as the leader, is to immediately begin living the vision. Suppose your vision is, "Let nothing stand in the way of making every customer feel as if he were the only customer we have." If a call comes in from an unhappy customer and you blow it off and decide not to talk to him, your vision will die, because your folks see that you don't walk the walk. Your associates have to see that you actually live the vision. Anything else is a recipe for failure.

Your next task regarding the vision is to remove all barriers that might prevent your associates from responding to the vision. Be sure your corporate policies do not set up any roadblocks that make it difficult for your associates to live within the vision. When you hold yourself and your associates accountable for consistently living the vision, your associates are serving the vision and not the leader. When you achieve that, you can declare vision victory.

Serving Customers at a Higher Level

In Enterprises of Excellence, everything starts and ends with the customer. These organizations evaluate every aspect of how well they are doing from the customer's point of view. All processes are designed with the customer in mind.

Both management and employees are accountable to the customer. This means that customer-facing employees can make decisions on the spot. And management has regular face-to-face contact with customers—not only the happy customers, but also those who are frustrated, angry, or simply not using the company's services.

Nordstrom's Department Store is a pioneer in the creation of "raving fans." Their core ideology of "service to the customer above all else" has been a way of life long before people even started talking about customer-service programs. Their planning starts with the customer, and execution focuses on the customer. Everything they do culminates in the ultimate customer experience. And look at what it has done for them: Nordstrom's has gone from a single shoestore in 1901 to 187 stores today in 28 states with revenues of over $8 billion. Unlike many companies who hire people with good sales skills and then try to teach them customer relation skills, Nordstrom's hires "naturally nice" people and teaches them to sell. Their "hire the smile and train the skill approach" works.

Not long ago, Nordstrom replaced its twenty-page rule book with a one-page sheet and these words of wisdom: "Use your best judgment in all situations," and "Do whatever it takes to make the customer happy." So a key aspect of new sales associates' orientation at Nordstrom's is learning how to say, "No problem," and mean it. And Nordstrom's employees can follow through on this promise because they're actually empowered to always use their best judgment. That takes some real courage on the part of management. Good judgment can mean different things to different people, and management has to be willing to allow their sales associates the right to make mistakes.

Combining the service ethic with best judgment has resulted in legendary stories of clothes being pressed, Macy's packages being wrapped, clothes being personally delivered, and two different-sized shoes being sold as a pair to fit a customer's different-sized feet. Customers are dedicated to Nordstrom's with almost as much passion as Nordstrom's long-term employees, who enjoy a generous profit-sharing contribution year after year.

If you want your company to be the Nordstrom's of your industry, here are five secrets to treating your customers right and turning them into raving fans:

1. Decide what you want your customer experience to be.

If you want to create raving fans, you don't just announce it—you have to plan for it, just like Nordstrom's did. What kind of experience do you want your customers to have as they interact with every part of your company? While some people will start by asking the customer what they want—and you should talk to your customers—the starting point has to begin with leadership. The customer does not know what the big picture is. He does not know what is possible. As a leader, you do. Picture what your organization would look like if everything worked perfectly. World-class athletes often picture themselves breaking a world record, pitching a perfect game, or breaking free for a ninety-nine-yard punt return. They know that power comes from having a clear mental image of their best potential performance.

2. Discover what your customers want.

After you define what you want the customer experience to be, it's important to discover any suggestions your customers may have that will make their experience with your company better, more enjoyable, or more effective. But don't just ask them a simple "yes or no" question. Ask them what you could have done to make their experience with you better.

You will often be surprised by what is really important to your customers. While working with one of my grocery-store clients, I asked the owner what he thought the most important thing was to his customers. Keep in mind that this was a thirty-five-year-old man who grew up in the business. If anybody knew what was important to his customers, you would think that he would. The owner immediately told me that price was their only consideration and that anything else would be unimportant. Now I had observed his customers as they shopped in the store, and that just didn't ring true. I told him I was going to walk through the store with some of his customers, and if price was number one on their hit parade, I would buy him dinner at the most expensive restaurant in town. If I was right, and it was something other than price, he would do the same for me.

I introduced myself to a couple dozen of his customers who seemed to be a good cross-section of his customer base and walked the store with them while they were shopping. I asked each of them what, in their mind, would constitute the perfect grocery shopping experience. Number one—by a resounding majority—was getting through the checkout counter promptly and not having the checkers talk to one another while they were waiting on customers. Number two was having a good variety of products to choose from. Price was a distant fifth. The owner was shocked, but we immediately took steps to make sure customers were checked out quickly and that checkers focused only on the customer. As always, knowledge is power. And of course, dinner was wonderful.

So learn to listen to your customer. When a customer tells you something, you have to listen without getting defensive—particularly if you've made a mistake with the customer. Defending what you've done will only irritate the customer. It is vital that you or your staff listen to the customer in a non-defensive, attentive way, and then ask, "Please tell me what we can do to win back your loyalty." Only after you've listened fully to the customer do you decide what, if anything, you want to do about what you have heard.

A perfect example of what not to do may have been seen in the late Steve Jobs' press conference to address the problems with the iPhone 4. This really mystified me, because Mr. Jobs had proven to be a master at dealing with the press and the public. But in this case, he never truly apologized or made clear that he was going to do whatever it took to win public trust back. Instead, he used a lot of statistics to show that a very small percentage of the phone owners had complained (likely because the press was reporting the phone's problems daily, including the fact that *Consumer Reports* would not recommend it). The closest to an apology I heard was, "No company is perfect and no phone is perfect." He also disclosed that they would provide a signal-improving bumper case to everyone who had purchased the phone. I have no question that if he had made a true apology in addition to the bumper-case solution, the public would have embraced him and his solution. After all, who can turn away from a sincere apology?

3. Discover what your customers think about you.

Customers want to know that their opinion counts. An effective evaluation procedure, such as a customer satisfaction survey, provides the means for customers to communicate their view of the company to management. A customer satisfaction survey is a great way to let your customer know you want to listen and you care about what he thinks. It also allows the business owner to evaluate the customer's perception of the company, its products, and its personnel. It is imperative that management take advantage of this information and constantly commit to increase the customer rating. One of the ways to ensure that improvement takes place is to use the customer satisfaction survey as one of the quantitative measurement goals for as many customer-facing employees as possible. (You'll learn more about quantitative measurement goals in chapters 12 and 13.)

A customer satisfaction survey should have the following principle objectives:

1. Measuring the customer's evaluation of how management and employees are performing their jobs.
2. Identifying weaknesses from the customer's point of view to drive improvement in these areas.

The evaluations should be mailed to customers ranging from twice a year to once a month. The survey form will ask the customer to mail the survey back to the customer in either a stamped, self-addressed envelope or on a postage-prepaid postcard. Many of my clients have chosen the postage-prepaid postcard, and recently some of my clients have utilized their websites to host their customer satisfaction survey. Management should share with all employees the results of these surveys, as well as any comments, and continue to be involved in frequent, informal discussions about the needed improvements with employees on a day-to-day basis.

This process is vital if you really want to know what your customer thinks and use that knowledge as a springboard to creating a better, more customer-friendly company. On page 79 you will find a sample of what the survey should look like, which happens to be for a service company. You, of course, will modify your survey to reflect the characteristics of your company.

XYZ COMPANY
Customer Satisfaction Survey

••

Please use the enclosed postage paid envelope to send back the completed survey.

Company_____   Job Name_____

Contact Name_____   Date Survey Sent _____

Just check the box in the survey form that accurately describes our performance in each of the areas.
10 is the highest rating and 1 is the lowest rating.

	1	2	3	4	5	6	7	8	9	10
When we completed the job and left the job site, we left the job site in the best possible condition. (clear of scrap material & debris)	☐	☐	☐	☐	☐	☐	☐	☐	☐	☐
Your rating of our level of dependability (Can you count on us to complete our part of the project within the projected time frame?)	☐	☐	☐	☐	☐	☐	☐	☐	☐	☐
Our billing is accurate.	☐	☐	☐	☐	☐	☐	☐	☐	☐	☐
Our Estimators responded in a timely and accurate manner.	☐	☐	☐	☐	☐	☐	☐	☐	☐	☐
Our Superintendents & Construction Manager are courteous & responsive.	☐	☐	☐	☐	☐	☐	☐	☐	☐	☐
We made it easy to do business with us.	☐	☐	☐	☐	☐	☐	☐	☐	☐	☐
We truly satisfied you with the quality of our work.	☐	☐	☐	☐	☐	☐	☐	☐	☐	☐
We are courteous & responsive when you call our office.	☐	☐	☐	☐	☐	☐	☐	☐	☐	☐

May we use you as a reference?   ☐Yes ☐No   Would you recommend us? ☐Yes ☐No

Please comment on any areas that need improvement.

_____

_____

Would you like to be contacted by our executive staff about this survey or any other matter?
☐Yes ☐No

Thank you for taking the time to complete this survey.

Prepared by Profitability Partners, Inc.
March 27, 2008

Figure 7.1. Sample Customer Satisfaction Survey

4.Deliver your ideal customer service experience, plus a little bit more.

Now that you have a clear picture of the experience you want your customers to have—the experience that will satisfy and delight them and put smiles on their faces—you have to figure out how to get your people excited about delivering this experience, plus a little bit more.

One of the responsibilities of senior leadership is to provide a strong vision of what excellent customer service looks like. Now you have to implement the experience. In the typical organization, most employees focus their energy on making the bosses happy rather than caring for the customer. Delivering this type of customer experience hinges on whether you can equip people throughout the organization to act and feel like owners of the vision.

A perfect example of this took place in one of Houston's best white-tablecloth restaurants. I dined there often, and the maître d' would often make a special Strawberries Romanoff dessert for my table. One day I took a client to the restaurant and bragged about the dessert, telling him to be sure to save room, because this is something he can only get at this restaurant and only if he is with me. So we finished dinner and the maître d' came to our table to inquire about dessert. I ordered the Romanoff. He apologized profusely and told me that they had run out of strawberries, and he asked what else he could bring me. I told him that I had really come there for his dessert, as did my client, and was really disappointed. He asked if I had about twenty minutes so that he could work a miracle. I told him to bring it on. He took it upon himself to go to a store that carried fresh berries, brought them back, and made one of his classic desserts. He hadn't asked permission to do that. He just took it upon himself to deliver the ideal customer service, plus 1 percent. He could do that because the owner had set up the organization to empower every employee right down to the dishwashers to make decisions, to use their brains, and be what Herb Keleher of Southwest Airlines called "customer maniacs" so that they could create raving fans. I love that term, "customer maniacs." Let's plan to be a company of customer maniacs.

So now you have delivered the ideal customer experience, plus 1 percent. You have just one more step—it is both simple and pure dynamite. **Thank your customers.** I have a client in the service business, and we recently decided they should thank their customers.

We had very plain, simple thank-you notes printed up, and we asked each technician to send a thank-you note to every customer for whom they provided service. There was a place on the note for the technician to write a personal note, which they all did. They tended to write something simple, like "Thank you for being so nice to me," or "Thank you for bringing me a glass of water." But the result was incredible. We received great comments from our customers. They invariably told us that no service provider had ever done that before. And do you know what else they did? They told their friends. We were the talk of our service area. This just shows you that the simplest action, done in a sincere manner, can provide unimaginable results.

5. Equip employees to deliver ideal customer experiences.

Finally, creating raving fans requires gung-ho employees. You cannot do this with uncommitted people. Here are three requirements for developing customer maniacs in any organization:

1. People need to have work that they can see is worthwhile. An old John Conlee country song has the lyrics, "From Monday to Friday, I sell my time; they just want my body, they don't want my mind." What a long, dreary life that would be. Worthwhile work gets people up in the morning with a spring in their step.
2. People need to be in control of achieving the goal. When people know why they are working and where they are going, they want to bring their brains to work. Being responsible demands people's best and allows them to learn and act like owners.
3. To continue to generate energy, people need to cheer each other on. There is real power when people catch each other doing things right.

Empowering Your Workforce

How do Enterprises of Excellence beat the competition on a regular basis? We just finished learning that they must develop a compelling vision and treat their customers right. But they can only do these things if they have a workforce that is really turned on about their vision and highly motivated to serve customers at a higher level. The key to creating this motivated workforce is *empowerment*.

Empowerment means allowing people to utilize their intellect, knowledge, experience, and motivation in the workplace, which creates the atmosphere that allows you to live out your vision and serve customers at the higher level. Leaders of these Enterprises of Excellence know that empowering people creates great results that are just not possible when all the authority rests with the Grand Poobah and drone managers are asked to take all of the responsibility for success. An executive of a large publicly traded company was obviously working in a Grand Poobah environment when he defined teamwork as "a lot of people doing what I say."

Empowerment is the catalyst that unleashes the power in people—their knowledge, experience, and motivation—and focuses that power to achieve great results for the organization. Creating a culture of empowerment consists of only a few key steps, yet because they challenge most people's assumptions, these steps are often difficult for managers and direct-reports alike.

Empowerment requires a very real shift in attitude, and the most crucial place this shift must occur is in the hearts and minds of every leader. If you ask an uninformed manager to describe empowerment to you, you will likely hear that it is "giving people the power to make decisions." This misguided view explains why so many companies have problems engaging the hearts and minds of their folk. This definition still regards the manager as the "big kahuna" and misses the essential point, namely that people already possess a great deal of power that resides in their knowledge, experience, and internal motivation. The enlightened manager will tell you that empowerment is the creation of an organizational climate that *releases* the knowledge, experience, and motivation that reside in people.

Direct-reports can also miss the point. Many of them believe empowerment means they will be given free rein to do as they please and make all the key decisions about their jobs. Direct-reports often fail to understand that there is a price for freedom, and that price is a sharing of risks and responsibilities.

While there is a learning curve from the old-style, "big kahuna" culture to an empowerment culture, the benefits can be well worth the effort, as we can see from the following case study about how empowerment was born in North America.

First, let's set the stage. During the 1850s gold rush in California, work habits from two continents collided. The Chinese brought worker-responsibility leadership to California, while the old-style, controlling leadership came from the eastern United States. How efficient were the Chinese with their self-management? Well, so efficient that the United States made it illegal for them to seek jobs or enter into businesses that Americans might want. So the Chinese reopened gold mines abandoned by the Americans and made them profitable.

Now let's move ahead to 1864, when the Central Pacific Railroad Company was struggling to lay track efficiently as they expanded the railroad from Sacramento, California into the Sierra Mountains. Someone at Central Pacific had observed how efficient the Chinese workers were at laying track. The company decided to experiment with a Chinese construction crew. Not only did they hire Chinese workers, but company managers also did the unheard of (by American standards) by adopting the worker-responsibility style of the Chinese, giving full control of the project to front-line work teams. As a result, track laying increased until it reached a record ten miles in one day. The worker-responsibility concept was so successful that most railroad construction companies adopted it.

Why did the worker-responsibility system work? First, the company had an incentive to try something new. The railroad owners knew that the old ways were not working, and they also knew that there could be no profit until the trains could run. These owners had to overcome their own class prejudices and actually ask workers for advice rather than tell them what to do. Making the workers responsible, or empowered, greatly increased the workers' intensity of motivation. In other words, they behaved like owners because they took on the job of improving the production, and that is exactly what you want to achieve.

The Keys to Empowerment

Share Information with Everyone

If you want your employees to have the same empowerment as these pioneers of motivation, the first key is to *share information with everyone.* Remember, knowledge is power. Making information easily available to your people is one of the best ways to build their own sense of trust and responsibility. In the old style of management, the big kahuna jealously guards all information and is known for playing his cards close to his chest. Giving team members the information they need enables them to make good business decisions. Sharing information sometimes means disclosing stuff that would previously have been considered privileged or divulged on a strict need-to-know basis, including sensitive and important topics such as future business plans, financial data, and problem areas. Yes, it is okay to tell your team that there are problems. Providing people with more complete information communicates trust and a sense of "we're in this together."

I saw a clear demonstration of this when I was helping to turn around a large franchisor that was hemorrhaging money. It was awful. Paychecks were bouncing. There had been layoffs, and more were anticipated. Rumors of impending doom were rampant. Morale was as low as it could get. The first thing I did was to call a meeting of all employees. I decided to take a chance and really lay out all of the facts. I told them what our cash shortage was and what the projected shortage was. I told them that we may lose 20 percent of the franchisees. But I also told them that I had a plan, and that if it worked, we would have one more round of layoffs within the next week. But after that, whoever was there was safe. If all worked well, their paychecks would even clear. If I could stop the franchisees from jumping ship, I thought the company was salvageable.

You know, I really didn't deliver great news to them. But I heard a collective sigh of relief, and each one of them told me that they would do whatever it would take to help. Several of them already had some great ideas to keep the franchisees. By having access to information that helped them understand the big picture, they were able to better appreciate how their contributions fit in and how their behavior impacted other aspects of the organization. All of this leads to responsible, goal-related use of people's knowledge, experience, and motivation. People without accurate information cannot act responsibly, nor are they likely to make good decisions. But people with accurate information feel compelled to act responsibly. (This sharing of information ties directly in to the Quantitative Measurement Process and the Pay-for-Performance Process, both described later in this book.)

Sharing information promotes organizational learning. Enterprises of Excellence seek knowledge by constantly examining their own environment, checking the pulse of their customers, tracking their competition, and checking the marketplace. They are constantly in motion, collecting information to make effective changes in their operations. Enterprises of Excellence also seek knowledge about internal performance. They treat mistakes and failures as important data, recognizing that they can often lead to breakthroughs. This is why Hewlett Packard's mission statement includes the statement, "We reserve the right to make mistakes."

This is also why every one of my clients holds a mortality conference after every job, project, or sale that results in a lower margin than planned or a loss. Mirroring the process that hospitals often utilize after a patient dies, all of the players meet to set out all of the reasons that the death took place, determine if it was preventable, and learn what should be done differently in the future. This is then incorporated into their best practices. After each of these "mortalities," my clients ask these questions:

- How much did we leave on the table in this transaction?
- What did we do that caused this problem?
- What can we do to prevent this problem from occurring in the future?

During this process, we encourage dialogue, questions, and discussions. Note that I did not say "recriminations." This "mortality" conference is not the time for management to take their frustrations out on the participants. It is a time to listen and learn. This process runs counter to traditional organizations where knowledge is hoarded. Enterprises of Excellence make information easy to access. Failure to do that creates barriers, which runs counter to empowerment.

Be a One Minute Manager

In his book *The One Minute Manager* (William Morrow, 1982), Ken Blanchard explains yet another application of the 80/20 rule: 80 percent of the results that leaders need from their people come from about 20 percent of the leadership activities they could do. Blanchard suggests three basic ways leaders can significantly improve their effectiveness in developing empowered employees: one-minute goals, one-minute praisings, and one-minute reprimands or redirection.

One-minute goals. Without clear goals, creating empowered employees just doesn't work. Continual feedback is vital. Many times unmotivated people do not really understand what is expected of them. And managers know what they want their people to do; they just don't always bother to tell them. To move toward goals, people need feedback on their performance. The number one motivator of people is feedback of results.

One-minute praisings. Once your people understand what they are being asked to do and what good behavior looks like, you are ready for the second key to obtaining desired performance: one-minute praising. Blanchard tells us that praising is the most important activity a manager can do. In fact, it is the key to training people and making winners of everyone working for you. It focuses on reinforcing productive behavior. Managers should look around their organization and see if they can catch someone doing something right. When you do, be immediate and specific with a one-minute praising. Comments like

"I don't know what I'd do without you" are too general. To be effective, the praise has to be specific.

After you praise someone, tell them how you feel about what they did. Don't be intellectual; state your gut feelings. "Let me tell you how I feel—I was so proud of the way you built that proposal." In this case, being close counts. You don't have to wait for perfection. When you see someone getting close to the goal, it is time to praise. Praise progress.

It is important that we make time for praisings. Two hours per week should be devoted to cheering people on. That should be on our calendar just like any other activity.

One-minute reprimands. Just as with one-minute praisings, one-minute reprimands should be done as soon as possible after an incident. Do not store up your feelings. Be specific. Share your feelings about what was done. "It really frustrated me." Remember, reprimand the behavior and not the person.

And here is the fourth secret of the one-minute manager: the one-minute apology. It begins with surrender. You have to admit to yourself that you have done something wrong and need to make up for it. A one-minute apology ends with integrity. This involves recognizing that what you did or failed to do is wrong and inconsistent with whom you want to be. Apologize sincerely, and again tell the person who was the victim of your mistake how committing the error made you feel.

Be a Servant Leader

This is another concept that requires a genuine paradigm change. Since the time of the Industrial Revolution, managers have tended to view employees as tools or cogs in a machine. We have begun to see a shift in that view. We are seeing traditional autocratic modes of leadership giving way to a different and more effective way of working—one based on teamwork and community, and one that involves others in decision making and is devoted to enhancing the personal growth of employees. Servant leadership emphasizes increased service to others and a sharing of power in decision making. Consider some common characteristics of a servant leader.

1. **Listening.** Traditional leaders are primarily known for their communication skills. Although communication is an important skill, servant leaders have a deep commitment to listening intently to others.

2. **Empathy.** The servant leader strives to understand and empathize with others. People need to be accepted and recognized for their unique attributes. These leaders truly embrace the Covey habit of seeking first to understand before being understood.

3. **Healing.** Servant leaders develop the potential for healing one's self and others.

4. **Persuasion.** Servant leaders depend primarily on the skills of persuasion as opposed to positional authority, and attempt to convince others as opposed to coercing them.

5. **Dreaming.** Servant leaders have the ability to dream great dreams. They understand the consequences of their decisions.

6. **Stewardship.** Servant leaders assume a commitment to serving the needs of others.

When people lead at a higher level, they make the world a better place because their goals are focused on the greater good. This is an old concept. Jesus exemplified the fully committed and effective servant leader. More recent examples of servant leaders are Gandhi and Nelson Mandela.

Use Your Time Wisely

We might all have the same amount of time in a day, but how we use this precious commodity is what separates the winners from the losers. If you don't learn how to manage your time, becoming a servant leader is out of the question.

In our explanation of questions 53 and 54 in chapter 5, we briefly discussed Dr. Stephen Covey's treatment of time management in his book *7 Habits of Highly Effective People.*

Here Dr. Covey outlined a Time Management Matrix that organizes our activities in four quadrants.

Quadrant 1. Quadrant 1 activities are *urgent and important.* This is the worst of the quadrants in which to operate. It deals with significant problems that require immediate attention. Urgent things act on us. A ringing telephone is urgent. Can you stand to allow a telephone to ring, or are you compelled to answer it? These items include crises, pressing problems, and deadline-driven problems. The result of operating in Quadrant 1 is stress, burnout, crisis management, and finding yourself always putting out fires. As long as you focus on Quadrant 1, it keeps getting bigger and bigger until it is your entire world.

Quadrant 2. Quadrant 2 activities are considered to be *important but not urgent*. Think about it. Isn't that exactly where you would like to spend your time? If it is important but not urgent, it means that you have the luxury of time to deal with an important matter. The activities that you will find in the second quadrant are prevention, relationship building, recognizing new opportunities, planning, and even recreation. (Yes, recreation is important.) While we react to urgent matters, important matters that are not urgent require initiative and proactivity. We have to act to seize opportunities and make things happen. In this quadrant, we do strategic planning and achieve results.

Quadrant 3. Quadrant 3 activities are *urgent and unimportant*. Some of these activities are interruptions, some telephone calls, some mail, some reports, some meetings, and popular activities. People who spend their time in Quadrant 3 spend their time reacting to things they *think* are urgent and important, when in fact the urgency of these matters comes from the priorities and expectations of others. The person who operates in Quadrant 3 is all about short-term focus, crisis management, poor reputation, seeing goals and plans as worthless, feeling victimized and out of control, and being involved in shallow or broken relationships.

Quadrant 4. Quadrant 4 activities are *not urgent and not important*. Some of these activities are trivia, busy work, some mail, some telephone calls, time wasters, and some pleasant activities. The person who lives in Quadrant 4 may be seen playing video games at work. What you find in this quadrant are people who are totally irresponsible, get fired from jobs, and are dependent on others or institutions for the basics of life.

The quadrant in which we choose to operate will determine how effective a servant leader we will be. Leaders who consistently spend their time in the quadrants of urgent and/or not important will never have the time to focus on developing and empowering their people. In fact, people who primarily live in Quadrants 3 and 4 lead basically irresponsible lives. But the question is, how do you get time to operate in Quadrant 2? Well, initially you have to take the time from Quadrants 3 and 4. You can't ignore the urgent and important activities in Quadrant 1, although Quadrant 1 will shrink as you spend more time in the proactive activities of Quadrant 2.

The whole subject of operating in Quadrant 2 is complex, and because of space limitations we can't cover it all in this book. So I'll ask you to do what I typically ask my clients to do whenever I am working on a project: read Dr.

Covey's book, *The 7 Habits of Highly Effective People*. To tell you the truth, I am not very big on self-help books. (Ironic, isn't it, considering that I have now written one?) One day my wife bought the book and, after reading it, suggested that I might want to read it. Being the type of person I was at that time, I scoffed at it, and I put it aside until we were spending a week at the beach and I ran out of all of the "good" books I had brought to read. Reluctantly I took it out and read it. I read it cover to cover without stopping. When I finished, I could not believe it was as good as I thought it was, so I read it again. It was a life-changing experience for me, and it could be for you, too.

I realize that you have had a lot to absorb. We've set the benchmark of becoming an Enterprise of Excellence, and to that end, we have explored the concepts of pursuing a driving vision and serving both customers and employees at a higher level. None of these are easy to accomplish, but with practice and effort, you will become a much more effective leader.

CHAPTER 8

Plan Your Recovery

Every time I meet with new clients, I ask them some standard questions to understand how their thought processes operate. Since you are trying to improve your business by reading this book and applying what you are learning, you too are a client of sorts. So let me ask you a question. Assume that two entrepreneurs, with approximately the same skills, the same industry knowledge, and the same capitalization, individually start businesses. In our hypothetical situation, the businesses are started on the same day. What do you think will determine which business owner will be the most successful?

The answers to this question always amaze me. Eight times out of ten, the answers I get focus on which business owner works harder and spends more time working at their business. While there is no question that hard work is important, it is just not the key to success. My experience has shown that the entrepreneur who has a well-thought-out plan and actually operates their business according to that plan will be the most successful. So keep that in mind as we begin to focus on changes that you need to make. You can work just as hard as you like, but if

90

you don't have a plan to achieve your goals, you will continue to feel like you are on a treadmill and getting nowhere fast. Truly, operating a business without an operating plan is like going on a trip without a map. All you can do is go and hope that you will get there eventually—wherever "there" is. The idea of developing a plan can seem overwhelming, but if you approach it methodically, I assure you that it can be done—and done well.

So where do we start? Well, first of all, we have to examine your vision statement. Or to put it in another way, why are you in business? As a rule, when I ask business owners what their vision statement is, I get a blank stare, and I usually discover that they don't have one. When I ask them the alternative question— what do they want to do with their company?—I usually hear comments such as, "I want to sell my products to customers," or "I want to make a profit." Surely making a profit is important, and it may even be part of your vision statement, but it really is not a vision statement itself.

As we learned in the previous chapter, an effective vision statement is one actively used to guide daily decision making. Let's develop yours so that we can go on with the planning process.

First, we have to create a vision that is practical and that works. An effective and compelling vision has three key elements:

1. **Major purpose.** What business are you in?
2. **A clear picture of the future.** What will the future look like when you achieve success?
3. **Clear and cogent values.** What principles will guide your behavior and decision-making processes on a daily basis? This would be a good time to go back to the previous chapter and read the section on Pursuing a Driving Vision, where you will see some terrific examples of vision statements.

The process of creating the vision is as important as what the vision says. Instead of simply taking the top management on a mountaintop retreat to craft your vision like it was the Ten Commandments and then announce it to others, encourage dialogue about the vision throughout the company. While the initial responsibility for drafting an organizational vision rests with top management, the organization needs to put mechanisms in place to allow others to help shape the vision, to put their thumbprint on it. For a departmental or team vision, it's possible to craft the vision as a team, although the department manager or team leader must have a general sense of the vision while being flexible enough to allow his team to alter his original position if necessary.

Regardless of how you initially draft the vision, it is important that you get input from those it affects before you finalize it. Ask people these questions:

- Would you like to work for a company that has this vision?
- Can you see where you fit into this vision?
- Does it help you set priorities?
- Does it provide guidelines for making decisions?
- Is it exciting and motivating?
- Have we left anything out?
- Should we delete anything?

Creating a vision is a journey, not a one-time activity. Communication is vital. You have to keep talking about the vision, constantly reinforcing it.

The moment you identify your vision, you need to behave as if it were happening right now. Your actions need to be congruent with your vision. As others see you living the vision, they will believe you are serious and this will deepen their understanding and commitment. One last task for you. Before you finalize your vision, go back to the previous chapter and review the vision statements of Disney and Give the Kids the World, and ask yourself whether or not your vision is as effective as theirs.

Now that you have your vision, it's time to begin to develop your operating plan. Let's begin with planning your revenue. Your first step is to look at your history. Look at your revenue for the past three years. Is your revenue up, down, or even? What is the trend? To calculate the trend, simply divide year 2 by year 1. Then divide year 3 by year 2. If your answer results in a number greater than 100 percent, you have a positive trend. For example, if year 2 revenue was $1,000,000 and year 1 revenue was $800,000, the answer to the calculation would be 1.20, which means that your trend was a 20 percent increase. If year 2 revenue was $800,000 and year 1 revenue was $1,000,000, the answer to the calculation would be 0.80, which indicates a 20 percent negative trend. Unless there are some very unusual circumstances, the revenue number that you generate when you apply the calculated trend to your most recent revenue year is most likely fairly close to where your revenue will wind up. Unless, of course, you take some steps to improve the revenue. And since you are reading this book, you most likely need to develop some improvement processes! We'll get to those improvement processes later.

Let's look at an example. In this example, the revenues for this company's most recent three years are as follows:

	Year 1	Year 2	Year 3
Revenue	$1,500,000	$1,200,000	$1,000,000
Trend		-20.0%	-16.7%

Figure 8.1. Sample Three-Year Revenue Trend

Note that year 2 reflected a negative trend of 20 percent, and the most current year showed a continued negative trend but at the slower pace of negative 16.7 percent. It would appear that, left unchanged, the negative trend will continue in the current year at a rate of about -15 percent. This means that the revenue in the plan year would be the year 3 revenue of $1,000,000 reduced by 15 percent, or $850,000. These results would be really devastating. Think about it. This company, if changes are not made, will have seen its revenues reduced from $1,500,000 in Year 1 to $850,000 in the current plan year. Does this sound like your company?

The next step in planning your revenue is to determine what you are selling and how it can be quantified. Whether it's a product or a service, every business sells something. Perhaps not enough somethings, but something that can be measured in units. Let's assume that you sell a product called a widget. You must determine how many widgets you sold in the prior two years and calculate an average selling price that should be effective during the plan year. Once you know what the selling price will be (subject to what you may decide as we plan your turnaround), you can determine how many widgets you need to sell by dividing your planned sales by the selling price for the widgets.

As an example, let's assume that you have determined that the selling price for each widget will be $85.00. If you divide our earlier figure of $850,000 in planned sales by the average widget selling price of $85.00, you will determine that the plan calls for selling 10,000 widgets. This is an important number, because now, in addition to knowing how many widgets you must sell, you know how many widgets you must buy from the manufacturer, or alternatively how much material you must purchase and labor you must employ to manufacture the widget yourself.

If, on the other hand, you sell a service, what you are really selling is your time, or the time of your employees. This is true whether you charge your customer by the hour or a flat rate. Let's assume you charge $100 per hour. You can determine through simple division that you must sell 8500 hours of your service to reach your plan of $850,000. But if you sell your service at a flat rate rather than an hourly rate, you must determine how long it takes to perform your average service. Let's assume that you determine that the average service takes 4 hours to perform, and you sell your service for $400. You will then divide the selling price of the service by the time that the average service takes to perform to determine the hourly sales price. In our example, you would divide the $400 selling price for your service by the four hours that it takes to perform the service and you will find the average sales price is $100 per hour. If you will divide the $850,000 by the $100 hourly selling price, we will determine that we must sell 8500 hours to reach our plan of $850,000. (That is, unless we find a way to reduce the hours that it takes to perform your service.)

Now that you know how much you are selling, you need to plan what it will cost you either to provide the service or to purchase or manufacture your product. The good news is that you have already done the work in the last exercise to determine how many hours of service you have to provide or how many widgets you either have to purchase or manufacture. Let's continue with our last example and assume that you sell a service, and that you must sell 8500 hours to reach your sales plan of $850,000. For purpose of this example, you have determined that your average payroll cost is $30 per hour and, once you add fringe benefits, your average labor cost is $40 per hour. If you multiply $40 per hour by the 8500 hours that we previously determined was necessary, you find that the labor cost is $340,000. You have also determined, for the purpose of this example, that you will utilize $150,000 in material as part of your service. This means that your total cost of sales is $490,000 and your gross margin is $360,000. So at this point, your plan will look like this:

XYZ Company, Inc.	2010 Plan
Sales	$850,000
Cost of Sales	
Labor	$340,000
Material	$150,000
Total Cost of Sales	$490,000
Gross Margin	$360,000

Figure 8.2. Sample Operating Plan, Stage 1

Now it's time to decide what other costs are necessary to achieve your sales and gross margin goals. Notice that I didn't say "make a list of your prior years' expenses and add a few percentage points to determine what your expense plan will be." Let's do it the right way. The only costs that you should plan (and incur) are necessary costs. So what is the first necessary cost? The answer is YOU! While most owners decide what their salaries will be based upon what is left, I am here to tell you that *you* should be the first item of expense. Go ahead! Drop in what you think you should be earning. Think about what type of salary you could command if you were working for another company. Remember, you are the person who most likely has taken on risk (such as personally guaranteeing loans and other liabilities), and you are certainly entitled to a reward commensurate with that risk. Otherwise, if you are just going to work for a paycheck, you can just go get a job and not endure the risk.

On the other hand, don't get crazy. I had a client whose revenue was in the $5 million range, and the three owners just could not understand why they couldn't make any money. Possibly it was because each of them took home a little over $250,000. The moral of the story is to be realistic.

Now that *numero uno* is accounted for, let's look at your other costs. For one, how will you let your customers and potential customers know that you are out there? You have to advertise. Let's assume that you will have to

XYZ Company, Inc.	2010 Plan
Sales	$850,000
Cost of Sales	
Labor	$340,000
Material	$150,000
Total Cost of Sales	$490,000
Gross Margin	$360,000
Operating Expenses	
Owner's Salary	$100,000
Selling Salaries	$ 40,000
Payroll Taxes	$ 11,000
Benefits Cost	$ 10,000
Selling Costs	$ 20,000
Rent	$ 20,000
Utilities	$ 5,000
Travel	$ 15,000
Office Supplies	$ 10,000
Advertising	$ 42,000
Total Expenses	$275,000
Net Profit	$ 85,000

**Figure 8.3. Sample
Operating Plan, Stage 2**

spend 5 percent of your sales for advertising. And now that you are advertising, you will have to have a salesperson to close sales. Like many owners, let's assume that you have a salesperson who you think is great, and you are paying him a salary of $40,000 per year. (The truth is that we would never pay a salesperson a salary. We will discuss compensation plans for your sales force in a later section.) Along with that salary comes payroll taxes, vacation, medical insurance, and workers compensation insurance. You will need office supplies and telephones and electricity. You most likely are paying rent. As you are planning your expenses, plan only what is absolutely necessary to conduct your business and achieve your plan. Your plan will look something like this (prior to us making some necessary changes):

Now that you've completed the operating plan, take one more look at it. Compare it to your operating results for the last several years. And then put it down! Don't touch it again until tomorrow. Sleep on it. The next day, show it to your most trusted advisors: your husband or wife, your top managers, or your CPA. Ask them to critique it for you in light of current economic conditions and your recent operating results. Tell them not to hold anything back. Who can you rely upon to tell you if you are off base, if not those closest to you? Digest all the feedback, and go back and revise your plan.

Now take this annual plan you have created and turn it into a monthly plan. Be sure that you take seasonality into consideration when developing this monthly plan. You can't just divide every line item by 12 to come up with a monthly number. Go back and look at your history to determine how the months will break down. Retailers often do 60 percent of their business in December. Heating and air conditioning contractors will do the majority of their work in either very hot months or very cold months. Just make this monthly plan as accurate as you can. This will forever change the way that you review your financial statements. Be sure that you insert the monthly plan into whatever accounting system you are utilizing. Virtually all accounting software, from QuickBooks to MAS90, incorporate the ability to insert a plan. If for some reason it doesn't, believe me, it will be well worth your while to change to software that will allow the insertion of a plan.

When you review your financial statements and you find a variance from the plan, be sure you understand why the variance took place, whether the variance is good or bad.

The key is you must develop a plan. Even if your plan is incomplete or imperfect, you are always better with a plan than without a plan. Just think about what it would be like to play football blindfolded. How in the world would you know where the goal line is? It is the same way in your business. If you don't have a plan, you are just running around the field, hoping to accomplish something. When you don't know what that "something" is, much less how to accomplish it, it's not only ineffective, it's frankly not much fun.

CHAPTER 9

The Harder I Work

I can't tell you how many times discouraged business owners have told me, "The harder I work, it seems that I just get further behind in the things that I really need to do," which is usually followed up by, "I don't know how much longer I can go on doing everyone's job."

If you feel the same way (and you probably do), you are not alone. Most business owners feel this way due to two main issues: First, they allow their employees to delegate up to the owner tasks the employee should be doing themselves. And why not? After all, who can do the job better than the owner can? This may be true, but if the business owner does not expect and motivate the employee to perform the tasks assigned to them, they are doing the employee a real disservice. The employee will never grow and thus never feel the joy of having accomplished his goals. Additionally, if the owner is doing everyone's job, there is no time available to spend on the really important tasks like strategic planning, analyzing ways they can improve business performance, or performing one-minute praisings.

When owners do not hold their employees accountable for the effective performance of their assigned tasks, they create an atmosphere in which employees tend to underperform and then wonder why they feel unfulfilled, which results in each day dragging on and on and on.

The solution to this problem is developing processes by which the owner can hold employees accountable, get them really involved in the business, and ensure that they do their jobs effectively and reach their maximum effectiveness. In this chapter, we will focus on using communication to develop accountability. Chapter 14, "Pay Your Way to Recovery," will concern itself with using appropriate compensation plans to maintain an atmosphere of accountability.

I find that most struggling business owners tend to play things pretty close to the chest and tend not to share with key employees the various successes and challenges that the company may experience. As a result, both the owner and the key employees feel isolated in the workplace. One employee in this situation described this isolation of non-involvement to me as "sort of dancing by yourself." The solution is to create an atmosphere of open communication between ownership and management in which ideas and issues are all on the table and freely exchanged. You must develop an atmosphere that eliminates the communication void. You don't want to operate like the former AT&T executive who was quoted as saying, "We know that communication is a problem, but we are not going to discuss it with the employees."

The development of that open atmosphere requires the establishment of a formal scheduled weekly meeting with ownership and all key managers present, to provide a forum for the presentation, discussion, and resolution of the many issues that arise during a work week. This meeting is intended to improve communications and, more importantly, raise the level of interdepartmental coordination, cooperation, and management efficiency.

Well-organized and well-run management meetings will have a direct impact on the morale, productivity, and profitability of your company. Decision making will be more timely and effective, since all key managers will be attuned to the current significant issues facing the company and focused on the same targets. Regular communication with their managers will help employees have a better understanding of their roles within the company and a better idea of the company's immediate plans and long-term goals.

Every company has certain functional areas, such as sales, marketing, warehousing, etc., each with their own disciplines and requirements for the orderly execution of their responsibilities. The need for effective communication exists at two levels: (1) within the functional discipline to foster the development of the required expertise and (2) to provide for the interdepartmental coordination of cross-functional cooperation necessary to perform as a team. *In non-consultant speak, that means you must talk and work with each other to make each other better!*

Standard agendas should be followed to enhance communications within and among these groups, keep employees informed and involved in the operations of the company, and ensure that management is functioning together as a well-focused team. The agenda can be amended as required to meet the information needs of the participants.

The purpose of the management meeting is to distribute important information among the company's key management personnel, provide a forum for free discussion and interaction among participants, and to allow for the assignment of action items by the chairperson.

These meetings will be held according to the defined schedule and be chaired by the designated individual. The chairperson will present and discuss any data relevant to this forum, and then the meeting will address the specific items according to the agenda, which will be addressed individually by the respective participants. All attendees should be expected to attend unless specifically excused in advance.

The chairperson must ensure the meeting discussions are controlled and do not wander from the meeting agenda. Action items should be identified, assigned to appropriate persons, assigned completion dates, and noted in the minutes for follow-up at the following meeting.

When discussing problems and/or concerns and assigning action items, the chairperson should keep the following guidelines in mind:

- **What?** What is the problem or concern?
- **Who?** Who is going to be responsible for taking on the action item to address the problem or concern?
- **When?** When is the action item going to be completed?
- **How?** How is the person assigned the action item going to resolve the problem or concern? (This should be determined by the person who assigned the action item.)

If an attendee does not have any important issues to bring up at a particular meeting, he should just pass, rather than waste the time of the other members.

The chairperson should designate an individual to take meeting minutes and distribute an action-item list to each attendee on the day following the meeting to assure that each participant is aware of any assignments and will be prepared to address them at the next meeting.

For these meetings to be effective and not degenerate into non-productive discussion sessions, the chairperson must enforce the following rules:

- **Never miss holding a meeting at the scheduled time.** If necessary, another participant should conduct the meeting in the absence of the regular manager. Meetings should be held when scheduled, even if all participants are not able to attend. However, attendance must be mandatory and any absence must be on an excused basis only.

- **Limit the meetings to no more than one hour.** Meetings consume valuable time, and that time should not be squandered. Continued extensions of meetings will lead to counterproductive sessions. So be on time, and end on time. One of my clients actually removed all the chairs from the meeting room so that the attendees would not get too comfortable.

- **Be concise and stick to the topic at hand.** Keep in mind that these meetings are to exchange important company information to ensure that everyone is aware of and is working toward the same goals.

- **Be sure to incorporate a Lightning Report** (you can learn more about Lightning Reports in chapter 10, "Know Where You Are at All Times"). Each person who has responsibility for specific line items must be prepared to discuss them. If they did not achieve their goal, they must explain why and tell the group what their action plan is to get back on track. This is not the time to let them delegate up to you by saying things like, "Sorry I missed the sales goal. Darned if I know how to fix it. What do you think, Boss?"

- **Ensure that action items are assigned to a specific individual and that a due date is assigned.** These action items should be tracked until complete.

- **Keep the meeting on track and moving at a brisk pace.** No side conversations should be tolerated, and everyone's attention should be focused on the person who has the floor at the time.

- **Insist that attendees come to the meetings prepared and on time.** Agendas should be prepared and distributed at least one day in advance, and anyone with a significant issue should give it to the appropriate manager to be included in the agenda, so other managers will be aware of the discussion to come.

- **Insist that action item dates be taken seriously and the required actions be completed on a timely basis.** Continually allowing action items to be deferred conveys the message that the actions assigned were not very important in the first place, and it does not matter if they are completed. Be realistic in establishing the completion dates, then stick to them.

Each participant contributes to the effectiveness of the meetings. The meetings are important to all participants, and each must convey that importance through effectively communicating those areas of significant concern that affect not only the respective departments, but also reflect the impact on other areas of the company and the contributions required from the other departments. For example, the sales department may be planning a sale on red widgets, and they need commitments from both the purchasing department that the red widgets are scheduled to arrive on time and from the warehousing department that they are properly staffed to receive the widgets when they arrive.

On the next page is a sample agenda that can be modified and used for your meetings.

We discussed earlier that the assignment and completion of action items are a vital part of the communication process. On page 104 you will find a sample of an Action Item Form for your use.

If you are utilizing this book to create change, your company is most likely undergoing a dramatic change in almost every area of its business, which will generate many questions and concerns among key managers and other personnel. Key managers will continually need to present, review, and discuss significant plans and issues. Only through constant communication and a generous allocation of time for that communication will the company be able to coordinate these changes and set a foundation for future growth, success, and profitability.

XYZ Company, Inc.
Management Staff Meeting
Friday, May 28, 2010
Agenda

Attendees: Mike Smith

                John Brown

                Brett Favre

                Mary Green

                Roger Bowen

                Sandy Steinman

Opening Comments: Mike

Action Items Update: John

Lightning Report: Brett

Collection Status: Mary

Quantitative Measurement & Tracking: Mike, John, Brett, Mary, Roger

Sales & Profit: Mike

Communication: Around the Table

NOTE: PLEASE BRING BRETT AGENDA ITEMS FOR EACH MEETING!

Figure 9.1. Sample Management Meeting Agenda

XYZ Company, Inc.

Action Items

Week of _____

Action Item	Assigned to	Completion Date	Comments

Figure 9.2. Sample Action Item Form

The bottom line: the management meeting's purpose is to encourage the active participation of all members of the management team, to discuss relevant issues and problems, and to develop solutions. Although it is not an arena to place blame for prior errors or omissions, responsibility and accountability needs to be set for the accomplishment of necessary objectives.

CHAPTER 10

Know Where You Are at All Times

I n order to get to where you want to go, you not only need to know where you're going (as we learned in chapter 8, "Plan Your Recovery,"), we also need to know where we're coming from, in terms of current operations.

In analyzing Question 14 of your business' Physical Exam, we said that you must receive accurate financial statements no later than ten working days following the close of the month. But is that all there is to knowing where you are? Somehow I have the feeling that you know the answer is a resounding NO!

The truth is that I want my owners to know exactly where their company stands well before that tenth working day when they receive their financial reports. If knowledge is power, then up-to-date knowledge you can use to make direction-changing decisions is a superpower.

Alright now, stop grumbling. I can hear you, you know. You are saying, "Look, I have made changes and have really stretched myself to get up-to-date financials, and now you tell me that is not good enough. You want me to have even more up-to-date information?" Indeed I do. "So how," you may ask, "am I going to accomplish that?" The answer is through a wonderful tool called a Lightning Report.

The Lightning Report is a report that simply compares key operating statistics to the operating plan and the previous week's key operating statistics. This snapshot should allow management to become proactive in resolving issues that surface as a result of this report.

The benefits of the weekly Lightning Report are:

- Creates a proactive rather than reactive management style
- Focuses management on key operating statistics by functional area rather than a sporadic view of the company in total
- Provides for the setting of goals that can be monitored weekly so that desired results are achieved
- Initiates communication between functional areas and management focused on common goals and objectives
- Gives each manager a view of company performance and the successes or problem areas that are being addressed
- Eliminates confusion and misinterpretation of company performance

We stated earlier that one of the key objectives of the Lightning Report is to provide management with a snapshot of the company's key operating statistics compared to the overall plan and to the same week last year. The size of the Lightning Report will vary depending upon the needs of the company. I have developed some Lightning Reports that are one-pagers, while one of my clients expanded their Lightning Report from five pages to twenty-five pages. Honestly, that seemed to be a bit of overkill to me, but it worked for him, and because he knew where he was at all times and could keep up with all of the other changes that were made, the company went from losing several hundred thousand dollars a year to making several hundred thousand dollars a year. So who am I to say that it was overkill?

If you are going to report on the key statistics, I suppose we better figure out what those key statistics are, as they vary from company to company. The definition of a key statistic never varies. A key statistic is one of the company's measurable results that can make or break the company. Some examples of these statistics are sales, collections, credit line available, sales presentations made, sales presentations converted, and many others. You can determine what the "make or break" items are for your company. One other thing: there must be a manager who is responsible for ensuring that the statistic being reported on meets or exceeds the goal that has been established. The most obvious example of this is the salesperson or sales manager who is responsible for the actual sales for the week, the number of sales presentations made, and the sales closing rate.

That closing rate, by the way, can be a real eye opener. I had a client whose account executive was closing over 60 percent of his presentations. That is really up there in the stratosphere, and it waved a big red flag. When we started to drill down into these numbers, we came to the conclusion that we were leaving gross margin dollars on the table. As a result, we dialed back his closing rate to a much more realistic 45 percent, but we gained about 4 percent in margin. This was one case where analyzing the Lightning numbers really paid off. There are many ways to develop these key statistics, and one of the benefits you get along with this book is a discounted rate for telephone consultation. Just e-mail me at sandy@ profitabilitypartners.com, give me your contact information, and ask me to call you to discuss the details of discounted consultation.

The Lightning Report should be prepared weekly, generally after the weekly payroll numbers are received. It will also include the prior week and the previous three or four weeks. It must be ready in time to be used as a focal point during your management meetings, as discussed in chapter 8, "The Harder I Work." All the information is gathered from the company's operating data. It is important to assign the reporting responsibility for every line of the Lightning Report to specific individuals (hopefully not you), and those assignments must be in writing. It must be understood that the deadline for Lightning Report completion cannot be missed.

I have included a Lightning Report that was developed for one of my clients in the construction industry. This is just an example. Remember, every company's Lightning Report is different, but this will give you the idea of how to construct a report that will best suit your operation. These reports should always be set up in an Excel spreadsheet, so as many of the numbers as possible can be automatically calculated.

Company XYZ, Inc.
Lightning Report
Bids and Securements
Week Ending _____
Page 1

	Actual	Goal	B(W) than goal	YTD actual	YTD goal	B(W) than goal
This week's bids submitted						
Number						
Dollar value						
This week's bids won						
Number						
Dollar value						
Backlog (won, not started)						
Number						
Dollar value						
Key bids in coming week	Due date					
Project name						
Project name						
Project name						
Project name						
Project name						
Project name						

Figure 10.1. Sample Lightning Report, page 1

Company XYZ, Inc.
Lightning Report
Week Ending _____
Page 2

	Last Week		Prior Week	
Payroll	Hours	$	Hours	$
Direct payroll				
Regular				
Overtime				
Indirect payroll				
Regular				
Overtime				
Total				

	Last Week		Prior Week	
Accounts Receivable	$	% of total	$	% of total
Current	100,000	50%	70,000	70%
Over 30	30,000	15%	10,000	10%
Over 60	20,000	10%	20,000	20%
Over 90	50,000	25%	0	0%
Total	200,000	100%	100,000	100%

	Last Week		Prior Week	
Accounts Payable	$	% of total	$	% of total
Current	100,000	50%	70,000	70%
Over 30	30,000	15%	10,000	10%
Over 60	20,000	10%	20,000	20%
Over 90	50,000	25%	0	0%
Total	200,000	100%	100,000	100%

Figure 10.2. Sample Lightning Report, page 2

Company XYZ, Inc.
Lightning Report
Cash
Week Ending _____
Page 3

Beginning cash balance	$0
Plus cash inflows	
A/R collections	$0
Other collections	$0
Borrowings	$0
Less cash outflows	
Payroll and taxes	$0
Vendor payments	$0
Subcontractor payments	$0
Loan repayments	$0
Capital payments	$0
Other	$0
Ending cash balance	$0

Figure 10.3. Sample Lightning Report, page 3

Remember, this is just an example. Create your own Lightning Report based upon your company's personality. And get your key employees involved in determining the key statistics.

CHAPTER 11

Sell Your Way to Recovery

C an you name a company that does not sell something? I suspect that you can't. Think about it. Retailers sell merchandise. Gas stations sell gasoline. Construction companies sell their skills. Even hospitals sell their bed space and medical services. So now that we have established this, let's look at how they go about selling whatever it is that they sell.

While there are a lot of companies today that sell over the Internet (you may well have bought this book that way), many companies have salespeople. These salespeople are all highly trained professionals and typically maximize every sales opportunity. Okay, I just lied to you. The truth is that many salespeople are poorly trained, incorrectly compensated, and poorly managed. If your business is going to get better, we are going to have to change the way your sales force (even if it is just you) takes your product or service to market.

I was at a client's facility recently when a salesperson came in to meet with the owner. I was asked to sit in on the meeting. This poor man (we'll call him Joe) was trying to sell cleaning supplies. Let me tell you, it was painful. Joe came in, made a little bit of small talk about the weather, pulled out his catalogue, and began going through it with the owner. He had no idea what his prospect's needs were or what might make him buy—nor apparently had any desire to know. After he had gotten through his list of items he wanted to sell us, he did ask for the order. I will give him a little bit of credit there. He said something like, "So, uh, what can I put you down for?" The answer, of course, was, "We really don't need anything, but thank you for stopping by. Please leave your card, and we'll call you if we need any of that." Apparently he was used to rejection, because he smiled and thanked us before he went on his way to bore his next victim to death. The next two sounds I heard were the door closing as the poor pseudo-salesman left, and his business card finding its way to the trash can.

Now compare that to another experience that I had recently. I was at another client's facility when a Yellow Pages salesman came in. We met with him. Let me start this off by telling you that I believe the Yellow Pages have become much less important than they were at one time, and to exacerbate this they have priced themselves out of the market in many cities. So as a result of my mindset, I was ready to make this a quick meeting and get about the business of helping my client improve his business. I was in for a surprise.

The Yellow Pages sales representative (very well groomed and obviously well trained) came into the office and, much to my surprise, began a very good sales call. He didn't make inane comments about the pictures on the owner's desk as he was trying to ascertain what the owner's needs were. He asked great questions. And these weren't just any questions; they were questions designed to make the prospect recognize that he had needs. He actually took the time to find out what was important to his prospect and how he went about making buying decisions. Then he proceeded to explain how his product (which included much more than just the print Yellow Pages) could enhance my client's business. By the time that he was finished, my client had admitted that he could use more business and that he liked what he heard so far. I am sure you already know the rest of the story. The salesman walked away with the order, and the interesting thing is he didn't really have to ask for it. He led us to decide that we needed the product, and we did everything but write the order up for him.

Business is really a series of processes, and the sales process transcends all industries. It doesn't matter if you are selling widgets or wind turbines, the process is the same. So while there isn't time to do a detailed study on the sales process, I will give you the short version. After the short version, you may well want to get more training in the sales process. I personally recommend that you look for your nearest instructor in the Sandler Selling System. These people have been well trained and really have their act together; in fact, it is by far the most effective selling system that I have been involved with. (And I've looked at a lot of sales processes.) Learn more about what they do, the products they have available to help you, and how to contact your nearest Sandler Training Center by going to www.sandler.com. I am deeply indebted to the great folk at Sandler for allowing me to excerpt some of the material from David Sandler's book, *You Can't Teach a Kid to Ride a Bike at a Seminar*, which has been extremely instrumental in the development of my personal sales skills.

I believe that their pain-based system is extraordinarily effective. Let me ask you a question. If you could create the perfect selling system, what would it look like? Sandler correctly contends that under the perfect selling system, prospects would:

- Deliver the presentation themselves
- Raise the stalls and objections and resolve them themselves
- Qualify themselves financially
- Thank me for calling on them

The system that I am going to present to you has several steps:

- Bonding and rapport
- Upfront contracts
- Pain
- Budget
- Decision
- Fulfillment
- Post-sell

Rapport. Sandler tells us that one of the things we ought to do if we are going to bond and build rapport is to be sure we understand what rapport is. The French often use *rapport* in the phrase *en rapport avec,* which means "to be in connection with someone." Another way to say it is to share a common point of view. The short rule for building bonding and rapport is to always make the prospect feel better than you. To a lot of salespeople that means coming up with trash statements like, "Pardon me sir, is that your sailfish on the wall?" Rarely do people say, "No I just found it in the thrift store and liked the way it looked." That kind of statement is for order takers, not professional salespeople. Don't misunderstand me; you want to open your presentation by talking to the customer and finding some commonalities upon which you can build. But here is a principle you should remember: *people are most comfortable buying from people who are most like themselves.*

To accomplish this, Sandler tells us about the science of neurolinguistic programming (NLP). Through NLP, we learn that 55 percent of rapport comes from physiology, or the body, and 38 percent comes from tonality. Only 7 percent comes from the words we use. In other words, NLP tells us to look like and sound like your prospect. Let's look at the things that make up 93 percent of the reasons that people buy.

First, physiology involves nonverbal communication. Unlike what many people believe, this has nothing to do with reading body language. Don't worry about why someone is sitting with his arms folded. All you have to do is sit the way your prospect is sitting. If the prospect's arms are folded, sit with your arms folded. If they are leaning forward, lean forward. Just mirror their physiology. You don't have to be perfect; just do it. You are not going to hear your prospect say, "You know, you look just like me, and by golly, I like you." But here is what is going to happen. As the prospect recognizes in his subconscious that you do sort of look like him, he will relax and feel comfortable being around you, and the barriers will come down. This is vital because every prospect sets up barriers, and barriers are the salesperson's enemy.

Practice this with friends or associates. Remember, if you can get this, you are halfway (actually 55 percent of the way) towards really building rapport.

The next step is changing the way you sound while you are talking to your prospect. Who do you think you want to sound like? If you said, "my prospect," you get the award. That's what you want, because just as people feel comfortable with other people who are like themselves, they also feel comfortable with people who sound like they do.

This isn't difficult. If you are talking to a prospect and he is a "soft talker," you become a soft talker. If your prospect talks rapidly, you talk rapidly. This is really important. If you are talking rapidly to a slow-talking prospect, your fast talking could lead him to the opinion that you are "just a fast talker" and probably too slick. Conversely, if you talk slowly to a fast talker, your prospect may form the opinion that you are a little slow and not be comfortable dealing with you.

Finally, listen for your prospect's favorite words and find ways to play them back to him. You can really demonstrate that you are on your prospect's wavelength and make him very comfortable being with you.

Before we get into the upfront contract, it is important that we understand why people buy—and this may surprise you. The answer is one word. *Pain.*

- **Pain in the present.** Your prospect says, "It hurts now."
- **Pain in the future.** Your prospect says, "It will hurt if I don't fix it."
- **Pleasure in the present.** Your prospect says, "This will make me happy now."
- **Pleasure in the future.** Your prospect says, "I can't wait to buy it."
- **Interest or curiosity.** Your prospect says, "That's interesting. Tell me more."

People make decisions intellectually, but they buy emotionally. It is important that you pursue nothing but pain. To do this, you are going to ignore everything but finding the pain that your prospect has and making him painfully aware that he is suffering. You must hit him squarely between the eyes with this pain. I call it "mining for pain." We will explore how you "mine for pain" just a little later, but for now, we want to think about the upfront contract.

The upfront contract says to your prospect, "If you have pain and you agree that I can fix it, you will spend the money to get rid of the pain. Furthermore, you are the person who can make the decision to spend the money." It is very important that you validate the contract. When I take the time to create this upfront contract, I rarely get surprised at the end of my presentation. Once a prospect affirms to you that he is the person who makes the decision, and if you can demonstrate that you can make his pain go away, he will buy from you. All you have to do is prove to him that, with your solution, he will be pain free.

During my sales presentations, I usually say something like this to secure the upfront contract (I learned this directly from Mr. Sandler's book, and it has served me well):

"Liz, I'd like to ask you some questions to make sure I can understand your business and to make sure I understand your concerns. You probably want to ask me some questions to see if we're the right company for you. As we ask and answer each other's questions, two things can happen. You may say, 'Sandy, I don't think you are the solution to my problem,' and if that happens, are you okay telling me no? On the other hand, we might be the right company, and if so, I would expect you to say yes. What I hope is you won't say, 'I want to think it over.' If you feel like you have to think about it, I'd rather you just say no. Are you okay telling me that, Liz?" Note that the one thing that I want to avoid is the stall of "I need to think it over." When Liz accepts that upfront contract, the odds are that Liz will give me a thumbs-up or a thumbs-down.

During our opening meeting, I try to involve the prospect. I will say things like:

"John, what are some of the things you would like to accomplish today?"

"Bill, I always like to know, what did my appointment-setter say to you that moved you to set up an appointment with me?" This reinforces the fact that at least during the appointment-setting process, he experienced pain.

Now we are going to explore how you go about mining for pain. What you are going to do is take a prospect from thinking he is okay, to hurting, to acknowledging sickness, to acknowledging that he is critically ill, to being ready for you to work your miracle.

Look for a suspect (anyone who is not yet a prospect) who says he is well. When I first begin speaking with business owners in sales presentations, most of them start out by telling me that they really have no problems. I know from experience that in most cases that is not the case, but being well or not having any problems is simply a barrier that must come down. Through my discussion with them (I ask a lot of questions, and we will discuss questions soon), I will find a problem and ask them how long they have had that problem. I have learned that suspects who tell me they have had the problem for years and years are not likely to become prospects. If they have had the problem for a relatively short period of time (say a few months), in my experience they may be ready to become a genuine prospect.

Change your suspect to a prospect by asking questions that will cause him to hurt. A "well" suspect has his barriers up and is not feeling any emotion. In his mind he is safe, secure, and, most of all, in control—and a prospect loves being in control. Your job is to make them hurt, and hurt bad. It doesn't matter, at this point, how good your product or service is. Until they feel pain, those barriers remain up. As you get more and more into the hurt phase, you will likely hear your prospect ask you if you can help. When I hear that, I invoke a process that

Sandler calls the Dummy Curve and say, "I really don't know. Can I ask you a few questions about your problem?" Don't rush. People buy from emotion, so they have to really feel the pain before the sale can be successfully closed.

Now make your prospect sick with pain. You have to probe. The more you probe, the more emotionally involved your prospect becomes with your presentation. This really makes sense, and you will more fully understand how this works as we begin to discuss the question-asking process and a process called "Reversing." We will also give you some examples of great questions.

Continue probing until your prospect recognizes he is critically ill. This happens when he is willing to pay anything and do anything to make his pain go away. Now you can show your prospect exactly how your product or service can take away all his pain.

When you actually follow the steps correctly, many times the prospect will virtually write his own sales order. Let me tell you about such a time.

I was in the middle of a consulting project for an independent grocery store. It was an interesting project. The owner was convinced his days were numbered because a Super Walmart was going to open within ten miles of his store. That was his pain. He was a great client, and by the time the project finished, he was more than ready to take on the giant. Because of the processes we implemented, he felt a 10 percent drop in sales during grand-opening week, and after that he was back to business as normal. One noteworthy fact was that this owner's father also owned an independent grocery store in another small town. He set up a meeting with his dad, and we agreed I would perform an analysis, which is a three-day mini-project, to determine if a full-scale consulting project might benefit his father.

I arrived at the store to begin the analysis, and the father reluctantly came over to shake my hand. We sat down and began the interview, which is part of the Business Physical Exam we discussed earlier. I opened by asking him why he was there. His response was, "Well, my son made me do this. I've been in business for forty years and I doubt that I need any help." In other words, he was well. I told him that I understood and that I may not be able to help him, but let's go through the three days and see where it winds up. The only thing I asked of him was that if we discovered issues that needed correction (pain), and if he was convinced that I could help him correct the issues (make the pain go away), he would and could spend the money to make the corrections. He agreed.

During the first day, I prepared a quick calculation based upon his financials and the comparative data available for stores of his size. I calculated how much profit he seemed to be leaving on the table each year. I saw that this had an effect, but he had no editorial comment. I just left that data with him and went back to work. During one of these analyses, I always have homework for the owners, and the first night's homework entailed his looking at his company's organizational structure and where some improvements may help. When he came in the next morning, he gave me his homework and said to me, "Well, perhaps we could use some help." My comment was simply, "We'll see. I'll know more tomorrow." I wasn't about to yank the fishing rod yet. He was now at the sick phase.

Through that second day, I spoke several times to the owner, just letting him know what I found and watching him suffer. Homework for the second night consists of about 100 problems that I found, which he was to prioritize in order of importance and indicate whether he could fix them himself or if he might need some help. In other words, I hit him squarely between the eyes with his pain. He could not avoid it.

When I arrived at the store at about 7:00 a.m. the next and final day, the owner was already there and, in fact, had a broom in his hand and was sweeping a hole in the sidewalk. His eyes were red from lack of sleep (due to an abundance of pain). I greeted him and asked him how he was. He gave me his homework and said, "I don't know what to do. I guess I haven't done much right over the last forty years. Will you be able to help me?" I assured him that he had done a lot right over forty years in that he was still standing, but improvement was always available. As to whether or not I could help, I told him we would decide that later in the day, when I reviewed all my findings with him (to show him how I could make all of his pain go away). Of course, I already knew that we would help and that he would engage us to help. Price was not an object, and he virtually wrote up the sale himself.

This entire sales process, when done correctly, is truly a beautiful thing.

All of the good things that happened during the three days at this grocery store happened because of the questions that were asked (both verbal and written). Let's explore the process of asking effective questions.

I guess the first question that we need to answer is: Is asking questions the answer? Absolutely!

Anyone who has studied the art of sales knows that during a sales presentation, the prospect must talk more than the salesperson. The problem is that most folks don't know how to make that happen. Sandler tells us that questions are the answer—not just any questions, but questions that make the prospect realize that he is in pain. Another benefit of asking questions is that you can keep the sales meeting moving. As I am sure you know, prospects rarely reveal their true intentions at the beginning of a meeting. It takes time and questions to get them to reveal what is really important to them. As we study this process, we will utilize a process called "reversing." Let's take a quick look at why using this process of asking questions is so effective:

- By asking questions, you cause the prospect to do most of the talking.
- Questions move the focus from you to the prospect.
- Questions flatter the prospect and show that you are interested in him.
- Questions help the prospect to resolve objections by causing him to speak out loud and make sense of the situation.
- Questions help you gather information, which leads to more questions.
- Questions probe and uncover the real issues that prospects may hide as a defense mechanism.
- Questions keep you from being blindsided and boxed in by a prospect's response.
- Questions allow the prospect to become emotionally involved.
- Questions help you to gain credibility in the eyes of the prospect.
- Questions help prospects solve their own objections. The truth is, only one person has the know-how and the wherewithal to solve the prospect's objections, and that is the prospect.
- Questions allow you to get information from the prospect that you otherwise would not have.

Here's how this process works. The prospect asks, "Will this home comfort system keep my home free from humidity?" The amateur immediately answers, "Absolutely," and misses a lot. The pro asks his own question and says, "That's an interesting question; why do you ask?" The prospect can now tell the salesperson more and says, "I'm just wondering if it might be good for allergies." The pro asks another question and says, "That makes sense, but can I ask why that is important to you?" Now the prospect reveals the real issue with his answer, "Because two of my kids have allergies and the doctor told us that humidity is not good for them." Notice the prospect ultimately laid out what is important to him (where his pain is) and now the salesperson can deal with it. Now that the salesperson knows where the pain is, he will most likely be able to add an air purifier to the order.

You can also soften the question by saying things like, "That's a good question. I'm glad you asked."

As the questions and answers go on, you may want to test the water by saying things like, "I get the feeling that taking the kids to the allergist is really beginning to be a problem. Is that a fair statement?" The prospect may affirm that it is a fair statement, or he may say no. Then the salesperson could ask what a fair statement would be. Whatever happens, the salesperson now knows more than he did earlier. Here are a few more examples:

Q. How long have you been in business?
A. That is an interesting question, you must have asked it for a reason.
Q. Is there an extended warranty available?
A. Supposing I said there was; what happens next?
Q. That's more than we want to spend.
A. That's not unusual; off the record, what were you hoping it would be?

I have from time to time been faced with a situation that I am just not sure I can handle. When I experience this situation, I will typically say, just as Mr. Sandler instructed, "We have a problem." The prospect usually asks, "What is the problem?" I then outline the problem and ask the prospect if he sees a way to overcome the problem.

One of the truths of life is that salespeople love to solve problems and to answer questions. But beware; one of the principles of successful selling is that you never answer an unasked question. For example, the prospect says, "The price is too high." That is not a question, but the amateur wants to explain all the reasons that the price is as high as it is. The right response is "Which means?" Now the prospect will lay out what about the price specifically is bothering him. For example, it may be a cash-flow problem where some financing will solve the problem, or he simply may not understand just how your product or service will completely eliminate his pain, which can more than overcome the expenditure.

Follow this example when the prospect says, "Your service is too slow." The amateur begins assuring the prospect that service will never again be slow and go into all of the reasons it is true. The professional says, "And?" Now the prospect explains the situation, and the professional knows how to deal with it to demonstrate how the pain can go away.

Another perfect example is where there has been some sort of unsettled dispute between the prospect and the company, and the prospect says, "I think this problem should be settled." The amateur immediately goes into motion to settle it as he understands the settlement should be. The pro says, "Settled means?" Now the prospect tells him what the settlement would look like to him specifically, and the salesperson can begin to make that happen.

One of the most effective "reverses" I have ever used is the "magic wand reverse." When I am in front of a prospect who continues to be a little evasive about his problems, I will ask, "George, if you had a magic wand that could produce the ideal solution and make your company look any way that you would like to make it look, how would the company look?" Now the prospect can paint a picture, showing how he would like his company to look.

Sometimes you will want to answer a question and then immediately reverse with another question. An example would be when the prospect asks, "Is there an air purifier system that works with this air conditioner?" The amateur says, "Yes," and then waits for the prospect to order one. The pro says, "Yes—why is air purifying of interest to you?"

Sandler teaches another process that you will want to use from time to time. It is called the "stroke-repeat-reverse" process. You will know to use it when you hear your prospects dig into their arsenal of "play-it-safe" words. What are play-it-safe words? They are words that will allow them to give you a little encouragement without forcing them to make a buying decision. Here is an example: Let's say you are getting towards the end of your presentation, and your prospect says, "You're close."

The amateur immediately says, "Thanks, Mr. Prospect. Then why don't you just sign this order?"

That allows the prospect to engage in all types of stalling techniques. Yes, prospects have their own processes, and many of them involve processes that allow their barriers to stay in place and the deployment of delay tactics. So the pro says, "Thanks, Bob. I appreciate that (the stroke). But let me ask you a question: what does being close mean (the reverse and the repeat)?"

Here is another example. Same scenario. The prospect says, "Well, in view of all you've said and done, there is a good chance we can do business with your company." The amateur does mental high-fives and prepares to close—which, of course, is wrong and will not be successful. The pro says, "And that business will certainly be appreciated (the stroke), but you said there is a 'good chance' (repeat). What does 'good chance' mean (the reverse)?"

Watch for those play-it-safe words. They may sound good when you hear them, but good things will not follow unless you deal with them properly. Some other play-it-safe words are:

- Might
- Maybe
- Possible
- Considering
- Looks good

Those words, and others like them, should trigger an alert in your mind. You should immediately move into stroke-repeat-reverse mode. Do not let your prospect take control by using that sort of language. Remove their "wiggle room" with this powerful technique. You affirm your prospect by repeating what he said. He knows you are listening. You are also asking for specific information to lead you to what must happen next.

Sandler endorses another technique that is very effective, but you better have the process down cold before you utilize it. If used improperly, you can destroy the opportunity for a sale. It is called "negative reverse selling," and in the hands of a professional, it is dynamite.

It is comparable to the fisherman who knows better than to jerk his line up just because a fish has nibbled on it. You know what he will get. An empty hook. The experienced angler waits until the fish actually takes the bait, and then he sets the hook in the fish's mouth.

The truth is, you can't sell anyone anything until they discover they want it. The use of this reversing technique can lead prospects to discover what they need and want.

Using this technique, when the prospect nibbles, the professional salesperson lets out a little more line. Instead of moving toward the prospect's interests, the pro moves away from it.

Let's look at an example of a presentation that I was giving for a consulting project. There was a prospect who knew he needed help, but he was really struggling to make the commitment to move forward. Still, he did manage to say, "I think that I could benefit from some of your services." The amateur salesperson by now would be almost giddy and would move in for the close. The prospect may leave him with an empty hook. Understanding this process, I rubbed my chin and said, "That's interesting. Based on what I've heard, I would not have thought you had a bit of interest. What in the world did I miss?"

Note that instead of moving in for the close, I moved away. I know this is unnatural, but the result was amazing. My prospect said, "I thought I was giving you fairly clear signals that you were starting to make sense to me." I replied, "Well, that's terrific, but I am still a little confused. Could you tell me more specifically just where you see the benefits to your company?" Now the prospect really kicked into gear and told me he needed the planning I was going to provide, as well as the compensation plans and job descriptions. He also liked the idea of making his employees accountable. He absolutely closed himself. He did everything but draft the engagement letter.

You have to remember to only set the hook when you are sure the prospect is buying—and even then, it would not hurt to try one more fairly gentle reverse, like "Mr. Jones, what would you like me to do now?"

There are a lot of different ways to set the hook. I have done numerous consulting presentations where I could tell there was real interest on the part of the prospect. Many times the prospect will say something like, "This sounds great. I think we ought to move forward with the first part of the process." Again the amateur jumps on that and brings the contract out for the prospect to sign. (Which may not happen.) Instead, I will say something like, "Are you sure that you have given this enough thought? Maybe there is something else that you would like to ask me before you decide to make this investment."

This really forces the prospect to close himself. Please practice this process. It is supremely effective.

There are a couple other things you need to know as you get ready to make more effective presentations. Buyers by nature want to create barriers and stall. They do the "buyers' dance." An example is, "Could you give me the proposal in writing?" By the time that leaves the prospect's mouth, the amateur is already working on getting it in writing. The pro knows that you never agree to do anything for the prospect without knowing what will happen when you do what they ask. My response would be, "Of course I can. Are there any parts of the proposal that you have concerns about? What will happen when I get the written proposal back to you?" I am looking for two things in this case. I am looking for the prospect to disclose his concerns, and I want a timetable for moving forward, not an indefinite stall.

You should also practice phrases that are known as "dummy-up" phrases, which are designed to make the prospect feel better about himself and consequently more protective of you. Sometimes this is referred to as the Colombo approach. For those of you who don't remember who Colombo was, he was a TV detective who was always very rumpled and ineffective-looking, yet he constantly caught the bad guy. His favorite tack was talking to the key suspect and pretending to believe everything he was being told. Then he would thank the suspect and turn to leave. But at the last moment he would turn around and say, "One more thing that I need your help with." Then he would get his man or woman. Here are some phrases that will help you or your sales staff become more effective and better closers.

- I forgot…
- Let me see if I have this straight…
- I don't understand…
- Help me…
- Tell me more about…
- Did you mean…?
- I don't suppose…

An example would be:

"I've forgotten, Ron, did you say delivery was important to you?" Or: "Sharon, I don't understand what you mean when you say you need to know more about the clauses in this agreement. Can you help me with that?" This invites the prospect to continue talking and helps you gather more information.

So the big question throughout this whole process is, how can you help your prospect discover their pain? It is done through active listening and asking questions. After the prospect tells you some of their issues, use words like:

- I understand
- That makes sense
- That's not unusual

Repeat or paraphrase the prospect's words. Say things like, "So, Don, in other words, you don't believe your current supplier is providing the kind of service that you need?"

Provide feedback about what the prospect is feeling. Say things like, "It sounds to me like you became frustrated when the promised delivery dates weren't met."

Here are some generic questions that Sandler tells us can lead to pain in a meeting:

- How do you feel about that?
- How serious would you say the problem is today?
- What were you hoping I could do for you?
- Is there anything about your present situation that you don't like?
- What are you thinking about?
- What would you like to change or improve, if anything?
- How do you see that working for you?
- Sounds like no matter what I say or what our system can do, it wouldn't make any difference.
- How long has this been a problem?
- What is the real problem?
- In the industry we have noticed a problem with...Have you experienced this?
- If you were to change today, what would you do different?
- Does that mean you are not open to new ideas?
- If you were to pick one thing you don't like about that, what would it be?
- Where do you see a need for improvement?
- When did you first decide you should look into...?
- Why am I here?
- Good. So what I hear you saying is that finding a better way of helping the plant get deliveries on time is not that critical. Am I right or wrong about that?
- How long have you been thinking about this?
- And you've never had a problem with...?
- How much is this problem costing you?
- How do I tell you that you're making the wrong decision without upsetting you?

How will you know when you have reached the point at which the prospect has real pain and that it is time for the fulfillment stage? There are definite signs and phrases that will give you clues, and you have to be attuned to them.

You must continue asking questions until you find the prospect's pain. A rule of thumb is you will have to ask at least three questions to get to pain. The first two responses will generally result in intellectual smokescreens. They are pain indicators, but not real pain. When you hear those, continue asking questions.

How will you know when you have hit pain? The prospect's responses will become emotional, not intellectual. A prospect in pain uses words like:

- Worried
- Concerned
- Frustrated
- Wasted effort
- Angry
- Upset
- Afraid
- Lost all hope
- Terrible situation
- Disappointed

Also watch their body language. A prospect may get up and walk around the room or look out the window.

Pain is not pleasant. Don't smile when you find it. Empathize with the pain. Tell the prospect that you understand, but improvement is possible.

Now move to the fulfillment phase. Fulfillment means to demonstrate to your prospects that your product or service will make their pain go away. Using the system designed by Sandler, you must examine some—or perhaps all—of the pain expressed by the prospect. As you go through the inventory of pain issues that you have uncovered, you should periodically take the prospect's temperature to determine how close the prospect is to realizing that the sale is closed. During the fulfillment phase, I will often say things like, "George, let me ask you a question. On a scale of 1 to 10, where 1 means that you have no idea why I am here wasting your time, and 10 means 'let's get the agreement signed and get things going,' where are we on the scale?" If the prospect responds with anything less than a 9, then I would ask him what it would take to get to a 10. At that point the prospect will tell you what you need to do to close.

Now the last thing you do is to protect yourself from buyers' remorse in the post-sell compartment. Buyers' remorse certainly exists, and the only way to prevent it is to attack it head on. You will want to say something like, "Ben, I know that there are other people out there who want your business, and I just want to ask you one more time, are you sure that this is what you want to do? I don't want you waking up tomorrow morning and asking yourself why in the world you agreed to move forward." Then wait for the answer. Once the prospect recommits, you are probably in good shape, and you have done all you can to prevent remorse.

This is great stuff, but until you commit to doing it and practice it again and again with your sales staff so that it becomes second nature, there won't be a real win for you. But given your commitment to change, you should be able to ensure that your salespeople adopt this process. If you want more along these lines, I recommend calling the closest Sandler Sales Process trainer. There are approved trainers near to where you are. Again, just go to their website at www.sandler.com.

The other important piece of this puzzle revolves around how you manage and pay your sales staff, as well as your other employees. We will address this in chapter 14, "Pay Your Way to Recovery." But before we can get to staff compensation, first we'll need to set employee goals, write job descriptions, and evaluate your employees accordingly—which is what we'll cover in the next two chapters.

CHAPTER 12

Goal Setting

I n this chapter, we are going discuss the process of setting goals. Because there are several levels of goals that must be set (corporate goals, departmental goals, and individual goals), it is vital that they be harmony with one another. Before we get down to specifics, let's look at an analogy that involves cell theory. Without getting too deep into the theory, we know that the intrinsic purpose of our bodies is to grow and flourish. And we know that the cells that make up our bodies are composed of amino acids. The question is, what in the world gives these cells, this bunch of amino acids, the ability to successfully accomplish those stated purposes?

According to cell theory, they do this by inserting internal control centers within each cell, so each cell can operate on autopilot, so to speak. This autopilot mechanism, deoxyribonucleic acid, is what we know as DNA. DNA is what makes it all happen—it is the transforming agent that gives the orders that control the functionality of the cell.

Just as the fabric of our cells is composed of amino acids, the basic fabric of a business is made up of the knowledge and the skills of all the individuals in the business, along with the business environment, missions, and visions. And the autopilot mechanisms of a business are the goals of the business and the goals of the individuals in it. It is important to note that some of the goals of the business may well duplicate the revenue and expenses figures that we discussed in chapter 8, "Plan Your Recovery," and we will use those goals to measure the overall performance of the company. The goals of the individuals within the company will be the way that we measure the performance of those individuals.

Goal Setting: How Business DNA Works

Goals are the transforming agents that control the growth and functionality of the individual employees and of the business as a whole, determining what the business and its individual employees will or will not become. There are several key components to making sure your business DNA, or your goals, are working well. First, *selecting the right goals* is critical (see chapters 7 and 8 for more on establishing goals). But so is making darn sure that the overall goals of the business are aligned with the goals of the individuals within the business. If that *goal alignment* does not take place, then the results will be like two people dancing, with one person doing a waltz and the other person doing a tango. There will be no harmony. Here is an example of goal alignment. Let's assume that the Adequate goal for each of your three salespeople is $350,000. ("Adequate" is one of the six performance levels for each goal—you will see that in a minute.) If each salesperson achieves their Adequate level goal (which is always what your corporate goals and operating plans are based on), your total sales will be $1,050,000. That means that if your goals are aligned, your corporate sales goal must be $1,050,000. So let's jump ahead a few weeks and assume that we have not only selected the right goals, but have ensured they are perfectly aligned.

After you have established the right goals and you are sure that the goals are in line with corporate culture and the company's visions and missions, you are still missing a key ingredient. What is it? It's executing the established goals. Someone still has to actually do the work!

If a company is going to be competitive in today's marketplace, workers need to have more intellectual capacity, more knowledge, be more creative, and have more ability to work effectively together as a group. So how are we going to be sure that our leaders not only ensure that the jobs actually get done, but empower employees to contribute individually while working as an integrated body toward common goals?

The answer is *goal integration*. To be sure that goal integration is successful, leaders must allow the visions and missions to flow throughout the company and be sure employees buy into these principles that drive the company. When this occurs, the company, its leaders, and its workers are bound by a common DNA. In other words, because every person in the company has taken ownership of the same guiding principles, the employee universe will be operating on identical autopilot mechanisms.

Goal Alignment and Action Plans

To establish aligned goals and create action plans to achieve those goals at the company and the individual level, we will use two processes:

1. Quantitative measurement (QM)
2. Goal execution

First, quantitative measurement helps determine which areas in the company to concentrate on when establishing goals and action plans, using the following six units of measurement:

1. Superior
2. Excellent
3. Adequate
4. Tolerable
5. Ineffective
6. Detrimental

Second, goal execution is a method for achieving specific goals. When you follow the goal execution process, you develop specific action plans; create processes to achieve the goals; and implement, monitor and improve those plans to ensure that you get the optimum results in the minimum time.

When used effectively, quantitative measurement and goal execution operate in business the same way that DNA operates within the cells in your body: they direct and process all important activities. Some of the activities affected are:

- Planning and mission-statement development
- Creation of goals
- Operating plan development
- Creation of supporting goals and action plans at all levels
- Positioning (coordination between the planned direction of company and day-to-day work)
- Accountability (ensuring that employees tasks coincide with company plans)

The real trick is to cascade the goals down to the lowest level and get everyone involved. The Ritz Carlton hotel chain has really gotten this down to a science. Consider their mission statement: "Ladies and Gentlemen serving Ladies and Gentlemen." Their corporate culture not only allows but insists that their lowest-level employee must act in the best interests of their guests.

I experienced a wonderful example of how well this works while doing a turnaround job in the Chicago area. I had to make a trip to Florida to meet with a prospective buyer, and I checked into a Ritz Carlton. I hadn't seen temperatures in excess of 20 degrees Fahrenheit for about two weeks, and believe me, I had one bad cold. The bellman took my luggage to my room and figured out quickly that my real plan was to pull the covers over me and assume the fetal position. About fifteen minutes later there was a knock on the door, and who was standing there but the bellman, with a pitcher of freshly squeezed orange juice and some fresh fruit. I was pleasantly surprised, but I told the bellman that I hadn't ordered anything. He told me that it would make me feel better, and it was on the house. What a great way to treat a customer. Just think about it. The bellman didn't have to ask anyone's permission to do that. He just saw the need and did it.

The antithesis of that story took place when my wife bought a dishwasher from Home Depot. After about two weeks, it was obvious that the General Electric dishwasher was just not doing the job. We could have simply rinsed off the dishes under the faucet and had them come out cleaner. My wife called Home Depot and was told that she was going to have to talk to General Electric. Isn't that great service? We buy from Home Depot, but they say, "Sorry, not our problem. Go call General Electric." She called GE, and they scheduled an appointment for a technician to come out and look at the problem. But then they decided to cancel the technician and told us that they were going to send us a thermometer, because before they send someone out they wanted to know what the water temperature was. No problem, right? We wanted to cooperate. The problem was they never sent the thermometer.

Up to this point, because of my travel schedule, I had no idea that this was going on. I was astonished when I finally found out about it. My first action was to call the Home Depot store and ask to speak to the manager, who of course was "not there." I was able to talk to a customer service representative. I explained to her that I did not buy the appliance from General Electric, I bought it from Home Depot, and I wanted them to take the dishwasher back, as I was within the 30-day return period posted on their website. I was informed that dishwashers have a 10-day return policy, and I was basically out of luck. But she would call G.E. and find out why they had not followed through.

After waiting another day, I again called the Home Depot store and asked for the manager, who again was not there. (I want his job!) I did get another customer service representative, and actually, in spite of the poor Home Depot customer policy, she turned out to be a great advocate. I explained the situation to her and told her that I was done with being put off. I wanted them to take the appliance back, and if they failed to do it, my action plan was to file a complaint with the Better Business Bureau and put my case on every anti–Home Depot website (and there are several of them). April, who was on the receiving end of that barrage, told me that she would like to find out what she could do to help me and that she would call me back the next morning.

Even though I had made up my mind that I would never hear from her again, she did call me the next morning and told me that while she didn't have the authority to do what I wanted, if I would give her until the following Monday before I started to take my various actions, she would make every effort to solve my problem. Sure enough, the following Monday she called me to tell me that she found someone in their home office who agreed that they would take the appliance back.

Just look at the difference in the way the two companies operate. One encourages their employees to do the right thing for the customer without asking for permission, while the other forces even a good employee like April to jump through hoops to do the right thing for the customer. Which company would you like to do business with? To Home Depot's credit, after I wrote a letter to their president telling him about my poor experience and, at the same time, what a good job April had done for me, he wrote me back, telling me that he had issued a special commendation to April.

Here is another example of what happens when every person is involved in achieving a common goal. I was a senior officer and part of a turnaround team charged with changing the performance of a publicly held restaurant chain that had about 750 stores. It was not a pretty picture. The company had lost several million dollars in the previous year. It was out of compliance with many of the loan covenants with its major lender, and they were preparing to tighten the screws. Worse yet, our profits had continued to fall. We had one last chance to succeed, and we knew that if it failed, we were done. Without being able to prove to our lenders that we had a viable plan, we would probably be able to fund about three months of payroll, and that was it.

First, some background. The company was made up of 600 company-owned stores and 150 franchised units. We knew that the company stores were doing poorly. They provided a poor product, and as a result they were losing market share. On the other hand, the franchised stores were flourishing. Their product was significantly better than that produced by the company stores, and as a result they were either maintaining or increasing market share. It was obvious to us that the difference was ownership. The folks operating the franchised stores had skin in the game, which drove them to excel at what they did, while the company stores just didn't have that motivation.

So we took our one shot. The entire management team agreed that our ultimate goal was to have 749 franchised stores and only one company-operated store that would be used for training and research and development. Each member of the senior management team agreed to take a group of stores and, within one month, franchise all stores other than the one store near our corporate office that we decided to keep. It was a major undertaking, but we set out on the journey. We sold some franchises to existing managers, who suddenly had some skin in the game as owners. Even if they didn't contribute significant dollars toward the franchise fee, they were on a note personally and were now responsible for making note payments and royalty payments. We sold some of the stores to a group of some of the top performers we called area distributors, and they paid a fairly large fee for their territory and operated anywhere from fifteen to forty stores. At the end of the month we had done exactly what we set out to do. We had 749 franchised stores and one company-operated store. We had collected over one million dollars of franchise and area distributor fees and had notes for several million dollars more. We were able to significantly reduce the company's overhead because we had now become a pure franchisor, which required much less operational support. In the first year under the new structure, the company had gone from losing several million dollars to making several million dollars. Everyone was happy, from the lenders who agreed to restructure the debt, to the shareholders, to the senior management team—who now had stock options that were actually worth something.

We had made a shared decision to pursue a specific goal with a specific purpose and a specific deadline, and it pulled together everyone involved, stimulating real results. It worked in that situation, and it will work for you too. Just remember that you have to create that same flowing effect:

Figure 12.1. Goals Flowchart

Corporate Goals

The flowing process begins at the corporate level. We have taken the corporate quantitative measurement goals from the sample plan that we developed in chapter 8, "Plan Your Recovery." Please note that the Adequate goal is always the plan that you developed. The quantitative measurement goals above Adequate (Superior or Excellent) will all yield more profit or less costs in whatever increments you and your team decide upon, and the quantitative measurement goals below Adequate (Tolerable, Ineffective, or Detrimental) will yield less profits and more costs—again, in whatever increments you deem appropriate. You will see the following exhibits below:

- Corporate Quantitative Measurement Worksheet
- Departmental Quantitative Measurement Worksheet
- Individual Quantitative Measurement Worksheet: Salesperson

If you will e-mail me at freestuff@profitabilitypartners.com, I will e-mail you the blank quantitative measurement worksheets for you to print out and use.

XYZ Company, Inc.
Corporate Goals 2010

Secondary Spokes	S Superior	E Excellent	A Adequate	T Tolerable	I Ineffective	D Detrimental
Revenues	>$930,000	$930,000	$850,000	$800,000	$750,000	<$750,000
Cost of sales	<$526,000	$526,000	$490,000	$468,000	$442,000	>$442,000
Cost of sales %	<56.6%	56.6%	57.6%	58.5%	59.0%	>59.0%
Gross profit $	>$404,000	$404,000	$360,000	$332,000	$308,000	<$308,000
Gross profit %	>43.4%	43.4%	42.4%	41.5%	41.0%	<41.0%
Operating expenses	<$292,000	$291,000	$275,000	$266,000	$308,000	>$308,000
Op. exp. %	<31.3%	31.3%	32.3%	33.3%	34.3%	>34.3%
Net profit $	>$113,000	$113,000	$85,000	$66,000	$0	<$0
Net profit %	>12.1%	12.1%	10.0%	8.2%	0%	<0%

By: _____

Date: 11/07/09

Figure 12.2. Corporate Quantitative Measurement Worksheet

XYZ Company, Inc.
Manufacturing Goals 2010

Secondary Spokes	S Superior	E Excellent	A Adequate	T Tolerable	I Ineffective	D Detrimental
Labor hours	<31,000	31,000	34,000	37,000	40,000	>40,000
Avg. labor hourly rate	<$9.50	$9.50	$10	$10.50	$11	>$11
Material cost per unit	<$14.50	$14.50	$15	$15.50	$16	>$16
Units produced	>11,000	11,000	10,000	9,500	9,000	<9,000
Defective units	<150	150	300	400	450	>450

By: _____   Date: 11/07/09

Figure 12.3. Departmental Quantitative Measurement Worksheet

XYZ Company, Inc.
Salesperson Goals 2010

Secondary Spokes	S Superior	E Excellent	A Adequate	T Tolerable	I Ineffective	D Detrimental
# sales calls	>550	550	500	450	400	<400
# sales	>275	275	200	140	100	<100
# referrals	>82	82	50	35	20	<20
Customer Satisfaction Rating	>9.8	9.8	9.6	9.5	9.4	<9.4
# days absent	<2	2	3	4	5	>5

By: _____   Date: 11/07/09

Figure 12.4. Individual Quantitative Measurement Worksheet: Salesperson

Developing Your Action Plan

Now you have your quantitative goals, and that is a great start. You are always better with a goal than without a goal. Now you and your employees must determine their current rating and develop an action plan to improve where improvement is warranted. For example, let's assume that the salesperson whose quantitative measurements are reflected above is producing sales of $98,000 annually, which has him in the Tolerable classification. It is your mutual desire that he achieve a Superior rating. You must now develop an action plan that will allow him to do exactly that. For example, you might lay out the following actions:

- Attend a training course given by the Sandler Sales Institute
- Practice your sales process at least two hours per week
- Increase your referrals by 25 percent
- Increase your closing rate from 50 percent to 55 percent

Those are just examples of what an action plan should look like. Once the action plan is developed and agreed upon, the employee must be held accountable for completing the steps set out in the action plan. That will ensure that each employee achieves significant short-term improvement, as well as achieving their long-term goals.

Now that your employees have goals and understand exactly how they will be measured and evaluated, it is time to go to the next step. This step ensures that you won't ever hear from your employees that they don't know whether or not they have done a good job. That's right. I am talking about the dreaded employee evaluation. Sounds like a tough assignment, doesn't it? I mean, you may actually have to tell an employee that he is not making the grade and has to shape up. It may sound frightening, but it is a vital cog in the process of improving your company, and it is absolutely the fair way to deal with your employee. So let's go on to the next chapter and find out how to go about this process.

CHAPTER 13

The People Side of the Business

O ften I have heard business owners say, "Business would be so much easier if it weren't for those pesky employees." Have you ever thought that? After all, employees can be unproductive, surly, greedy, and good grief, they are so needy! Well, guess what? Those employees didn't just show up at your doorstep and commence to torment you. *You hired them!* They are the product of your decision making. You thought they were good enough when you hired them, didn't you? In fact, you were downright euphoric after you made some of those hires. So, what happened?

Well, it is possible they were simply a mistake. Maybe you hired the wrong people. Or maybe they are just not motivated. You haven't found the way to keep them really interested in doing a great job. Perhaps they don't feel appreciated, or they might not know what you think of their performance. Whatever the answer is, you are most likely not a victim. Odds are the root of your employee problems can be traced right back to you, the boss. I typically find that employers make errors of commission and omission when dealing with their employees. Let's look at how employees often feel about their employers.

The Employee Survey

As a consultant, during an initial examination I always recommend using an anonymous survey to get a picture of the employees' perception of the company. It is amazing how honest employees can be about their perception of the company when they don't feel threatened. And things can get quite emotional when I discuss these issues with employers. I have seen emotions that range from anger to tears when employers are confronted with the employees' view of their company. This can be an important process, but if you are going to do this, you will have to engage an independent person to receive and compile the completed surveys, so the employees can be comfortable that you will not try to identify them through their handwriting. You can learn some important truths about the way your employees view the company and their jobs, many of which are actionable.

One of the most eye-opening surveys we performed was for a client in the manufacturing business. It was a fairly small business, and the owner lived near the production facility and typically brought her dogs to work with her. No problem, right? She loved dogs, so surely her employees felt the same way. Imagine her surprise when we got several comments back indicating that the employees did not like working in a "kennel." The owner's feelings were hurt, and then she got angry. But once the anger was gone, she began to understand that she could improve the work environment by keeping her pets at home. It was amazing to see the improvement in morale when she started coming to work without her dogs. The survey can surely open our eyes to things that just don't seem like a problem to us as owners, but really weigh heavily on our employees.

Just look at the average results of our employee surveys on the next page.

As an outsider looking in, what would your response be to a company whose employees felt this way about their employer? Wouldn't you agree that these are truly shocking results? And yet, if the right processes are put into place and the changes are made in an effective manner, the picture can change—and change fairly rapidly. Let's examine some of the issues in more detail.

Are Your Responsibilities Well Planned and Set Out in an Organized Manner?

It's hard to believe, but it has been my experience that about half of the employees do not know exactly what is expected in their job. There is, of course, a solution, which is simply planning your employees' responsibilities and setting them out in an organized manner. Here is how you will do it: Every job—and I do mean every job, from CEO to floor sweeper—should have a formal, written, well-thought-out job description. This should be given to the employee, and there should be a signature page to memorialize the fact that the employee has read the job description and understands the job description.

Employee Questionnaire Summary
(27 submitted)

	yes	no
1. Do you get cooperation from other employees when you need it?	60%	40%
2. Do you believe that teamwork accurately describes the company's organization?	52%	48%
3. Do you understand exactly what is expected in your job?	55%	45%
4. Do you always know when you have done a good job?	52%	48%
5. Do you always get the help that you need to do a good job?	59%	41%
6. Do you think that the company's treatment of employees is fair?	33%	67%
7. Does ownership completely understand your work problems?	44%	56%
8. Does management always listen to your ideas?	48%	52%
9. Is poor employee performance tolerated?	65%	35%
10. Does management accept your ideas?	41%	59%
11. Does the company move rapidly to solve problems?	33%	67%
12. Are your responsibilities well planned and set out in an organized manner?	37%	63%
13. Do well-performing employees receive better pay increases than poor performing employees?	33%	67%
14. Are your interests and ambitions being challenged?	52%	48%
15. Is the company changing for the better?	44%	56%

Figure 13.1. Employee Questionnaire Summary

Every job description should be structured in exactly the same way and should include the following sections:

- **The purpose.** Why does the position exist?
- **The duties and responsibilities.** What is the employee required to do to perform their job? Break down the duties and responsibilities into the smallest possible increments. Don't be afraid to have dozens of items here. Paper is cheap.
- **The reporting relationship.** To whom does the employee report directly? This should be the same individual who will evaluate the employee. (We will discuss employee evaluations shortly.)
- **The job qualifications.** What qualifications must the employee possess? What education level must have been achieved? How many years of experience must they have? What certifications are necessary? What language and math skills are needed? How about their reasoning ability? What are the physical requirements needed? How many pounds will they be required to lift? Remember, as you create the job qualifications, you are creating qualifications that you would like a candidate to possess if you were currently interviewing for the position. If your current employee is lacking some of the qualifications, you may want to help them obtain some of those qualifications. For example, if your written qualification calls for someone trained in the Sandler method, you may want to hire a Sandler-certified trainer to help your employee meet your written requirements.
- **The work environment.** What are the working conditions?
- **The measures of performance.** Upon what measurable standards will the employee be evaluated? Be very specific. These standards must be both measurable and quantifiable. (These are the quantitative measurements we discussed in the previous chapter.)
- **The job summary.** In two or three sentences, what is the position all about?
- **The acknowledgment.** The employee acknowledges that he or she has read and understands the job description and that it is accurate and complete. The employee also acknowledges that the company has the right to change the job description at any time.

Writing job descriptions may not be easy, but it is important if you want to avoid having your employees say, "I don't know exactly what is expected of me in my job." Why is this important? Because if they don't understand exactly what is expected of them, how in the world can they perform effectively?

The sample job description shown below is for a service technician at ABC Heating and Air Conditioning, Inc. This will give you a model to use as you construct the job descriptions for your employees. Be sure that you involve your managers in writing the job descriptions for the employees who report directly to them. Oh, yeah—one more thing. Be sure to write one for yourself. Remember we said earlier that you must have written job descriptions for every employee, and that includes you.

ABC Heating and Air Conditioning, Inc.
Job Description
Service Technician

I. **Purpose**

This position is responsible for the diagnosing, repairing, and servicing equipment and systems in the HVAC industry.

II. **Duties and Responsibilities**

1. Examines malfunctioning defined units for defective parts utilizing knowledge of mechanical, electrical, and equipment functioning theory to determine the cause of the malfunction.

2. Practices inspection routines employing the company's diagnostic procedures to pinpoint the area of malfunction.

3. Dismantles whole or parts of units as indicated by type of malfunction, and repairs or replaces such parts and other components using hand tools and power tools.

4. Reassembles unit, making necessary adjustment to ensure efficient operation.

5. Accurately estimates cost of repair or service employing the rate structure as established by the company.

6. Performs defined and qualified services that are at least 10 percent less than flat time.

7. Responsible for maintaining truck inventory and will advise service manager when items of inventory need to be increased.

8. Accurately completes all paperwork upon completion of service calls and accounts for all labor expended and parts used.

9. Drives company vehicles in a safe and prudent manner.

10. Responsible for the training and cross-training of shop personnel.

11. Stays abreast of the technical advances in the industry and attends all company-sponsored training programs.

12. Will present invoice and collect cash as required by company. Accounts for all cash on a daily basis.

13. Responsible for producing daily production reports.

14. Presents a favorable image of the company by adherence to the company's dress and conduct codes.

15. Demonstrates workmanship and skills by achieving callback rate that meets or exceeds the Adequate level as set out in the Quantitative Measurement.

16. Achieves Customer Satisfaction Survey results at least at the Adequate level as set out in the Quantitative Measurement.

17. Works in a neat and clean manner when working in a customer's home. Always takes all old parts or debris when leaving the premises.

18. Submits, in a timely manner, a report to management after any service call during which faulty equipment is observed that should be replaced.

19. Notifies service coordinator at arrival at job and just prior to completing paperwork at completion of job.

20. Perform any other functions as directed by management.

III. Reporting Relationship

The Service Technician reports to the Service Manager.

IV. Job Qualifications

The individual occupying this position must be an experienced professional who already has the training required for this job and has little need for any additional on-the-job training, except in the area of computerization techniques.

Education/Experience

- High school diploma.
- Five years prior experience in service and repair of HVAC equipment.
- Demonstrated capability in the diagnosis of technical equipment problems and associated repair options.

- Completion of EPA certifications and of specified vendor equipment training and certification programs as designated by management.

Language Skills

Ability to read, analyze, and interpret manuals, bulletins, brochures, instructions, etc.

Mathematical Skills

Ability to work with mathematical concepts and fundamentals.

Reasoning Ability

Ability to identify and define problems, collect data, establish facts, and arrive at valid conclusions based upon the available information.

Physical Demands

The physical demands described here are representative of those that must be met by an employee to successfully perform the essential functions of the job. Reasonable accommodations may be made to enable individuals with disabilities to perform the essential functions.

While performing the duties of this job, the employee is regularly required to sit, stand, and communicate telephonically and in person. May be required to lift up to 100 pounds.

Work Environment

The work environment characteristics described are representative of those an employee encounters while performing the essential functions of this job. Reasonable accommodations may be made to enable individuals with disabilities to perform the essential functions.

While performing the functions and duties of this job, an employee regularly works at customer's location and may also work in the shop.

V. **Measures of Performance**

1. Achieves attendance levels that meet or exceed the Quantitative Measurement Adequate level.

2. Achieves lateness levels that meet or exceed the Quantitative Measurement Adequate level.

3. Achieves Customer Satisfaction Survey results (both internal and external) that meet or exceed Quantitative Measurement Adequate level.

4. Achieves call back rate that meets or exceeds the Quantitative Measurement Adequate level.

5. Achieves comparison to flat time on jobs that meets or exceeds the Quantitative Measurement Adequate level.

VI. Job Summary

This position is responsible for servicing and maintaining HVAC and associated equipment for customers under service contract and for customers who contract for services on a one-time basis.

VII. Acknowledgment

I have reviewed and understand the above job description and believe it to be accurate and complete. I also acknowledge that management has the right to change this job description at any time.

Employee _____ Date _____

Supervisor _____ Date _____

Now that you have completed the job descriptions and your employees have signed off on them, you can sit back and revel in the fact that they can no longer say that their responsibilities are not set out in an organized manner. And that is a real accomplishment. But remember, we have to deal with the fact that they still don't always know when they have done a good job. So let's deal with that right now.

Do You Always Know When You Have Done a Good Job?

When I talk to employees about how they know they are doing, I get some really amazing answers. A surprising number of answers are in the range of, "Well, if the boss isn't chewing me out, I guess I'm doing okay." What kind of a working environment is that, where your only measurement of management's view of your performance is how often you get chewed out? My experience has been that business owners do a relatively poor job communicating with their employees regarding the employee's performance. This is unacceptable, because employees want and need to know how they are doing. Additionally, failing to let the employees know how they are doing violates just about every basic management principle. You must set aside a time for a formal, organized evaluation of each employee's performance. But before you can do that, you'll need to establish the basis upon which they will be evaluated.

Please read the Employee Performance Evaluation Procedure (shown below) that I created for several of my clients and begin implementation of the evaluation process. You will be amazed to see the improvement that will take place once your employees know how they are doing and what they must do to do better. Be sure to meet with your employees and let them know what you are going to do and how they will be judged. Once you have done that, you are now accountable to them for ensuring that this process is carried out.

One additional note. In the process outlined below, you will see a full explanation of how to utilize quantitative measurement to motivate and to reward your employees by awarding salary increases when earned. In the next chapter, you will learn how to utilize the quantitative goals in a pay-for-performance plan that will motivate all of your employees. Here is the Employee Performance Evaluation Procedure:

Employee Performance Evaluation Procedure

Purpose

This procedure lays out the guidelines by which XYZ Company will evaluate employees. Employee evaluation, which is in essence a two-way communication between employee and manager, can sometimes be misunderstood. It is therefore essential that the procedure used not only *be* fair, equitable, and objective, but *be perceived* as fair, equitable, and objective.

Introduction

XYZ Company recognizes that employees generally desire a periodic evaluation of their performance. An effective evaluation procedure provides the means for management to recognize strong performance. Evaluating an employee's performance is not an easy task, nor is it a pleasant one at times. However, it is the responsibility of the manager, in fairness not only to XYZ Company, but also to the employee, to evaluate and discuss job performance.

The experience should always be positive when viewed as a benefit to the organization as a whole. Even a substandard review can be viewed as positive to the employee if it provides him/her a means to improve skills and job performance.

The performance evaluation has the following principal objectives:

- To evaluate how the job is being performed and to determine what areas, if any, need improvement
- To assess short- and long-term potential
- To identify employee weaknesses, to enable the manager to seek ways to make the employee stronger in those areas

It should be noted that evaluation of compensation is performed every twelve months, while evaluation of performance is made every six months.

Managers should be involved in frequent, informal discussions with employees on a day-to-day basis. Progress is more formally summarized in the performance evaluation. Informal discussions establish the following:

- How the job is going
- What problems, if any, there have been
- What specifically may be expected of the employee over the short run

The informal discussion forum is a natural progression, culminating in the performance evaluation, and eliminates any surprises for the employee at the review meeting. The formal review does the following:

1. Communicates to the employee as to how the manager rates their job performance, and sets the stage for letting the employees know what expectations the manager and the company have of them over the next six months.
2. Allows the employee to comment on their evaluation and their future with the company.
3. Provides a permanent record of the review for purposes of career development, training, promotion, and pay increases.

Evaluation Ratings

The evaluation process is an objective approach and a constructive process, applied to each employee performance rating category. Care must be exercised to exclude the influence of comments or opinions of others who do not have direct interface or contact with the employee. The manager must use his/her reasoning and judgment in the evaluation process.

The evaluation must reflect the sum of all events in the employee's work history since the last evaluation. Single events in this history should be weighted in the total review for the period covered, but they should not have a total influence on the review. If the employee being evaluated is not a supervisor or manager, the eighth and ninth items in Specific Work Characteristics should be omitted. Simply average the score obtained on the remaining nine items and use that score for the eighth and ninth items.

The following factors need to be recognized as counterproductive to the evaluation process and should be consciously avoided:

- **Leveling effect.** Rating the employee the same in every rating category, based on a general opinion of their job performance. Each category must be evaluated separately and objectively.
- **Predisposition.** Allowing the evaluating manager's likes or dislikes of the individual to affect the evaluation.
- **Longevity.** Rating the employee on length of service rather than the quality of their job performance.
- **Projection.** Allowing the employee's personality, appearance, and work habits to project into the rating process on a personal basis rather than a performance basis.
- **Desire to please.** Giving a higher rating out of a desire to please and remain in a positive light with the employee.
- **Super-critical.** Rating all employees below standard because the manager may be a perfectionist and overly critical.
- **Insecurity.** Giving low ratings to an employee because the manager sees the employee as a threat and a challenge to his own position.

Preparing the Evaluation Form

Each employee has a quantitative measurement sheet. That quantitative measurement sheet must be thoroughly discussed with each employee prior to the beginning of the review year. At the beginning of the review year, the employee's manager must identify the five most important areas where the employee can affect the company's overall performance and insert those measurable, quantifiable goals, along with a detailed description of what constitutes each level of performance, into items 1-5 on the XYZ Company Employee Performance Evaluation Form. (In the event that an employee does not have five quantitative measurement items, the average of the measurable items will be inserted in the missing quantitative measurement positions.) While this is a time-consuming task, it is very effective in that each employee will understand exactly what standards they will be evaluated upon. Sixty percent of the potential maximum score is based upon the quantitative measurement standards, with the remaining 40 percent based upon specific work characteristics.

Evaluation

The scores resulting from the evaluation may be grouped in the following categories: Superior, Excellent, Adequate, Tolerable, Ineffective, or Detrimental. An overall rating can objectively be determined by applying the overall points scored to the following levels of achievement.

Superior (79-83 points). Achieves spectacular performance and superlative results. Possess the highest possible levels of expertise, competence, skill, and knowledge. Known for excellence. Is virtually error free, impeccable, and has no discernible defects or shortcomings.

Excellent (75-78 points). Achieves superior performance and above-average results. Clearly ahead of the pack. Has superior expertise, skills, and knowledge. Shows marks of Superior. Has a few imperfections, problems, or obstacles that should be worked on to improve performance and increase growth.

Adequate (67-74 points). Achieves adequate progress and results. Has several imperfections, problems, or obstacles that should be worked on to improve performance and increase growth. Meets all basic demands or desires. May show a few marks of Superior or Excellent performance, but not consistently or pervasively.

Tolerable (58-66 points). Achieves adequate progress and results, but sometime intermittently or barely so. Has a number of significant imperfections, problems, or obstacles that should be worked on to improve performance and increase growth. Meeting most but not all basic demands or desires. Not doing anything that is Superior or Excellent.

Ineffective (50-57 points). Not achieving progress or results necessary for growth or development. In a declining or otherwise undesirable state. Has many significant imperfections, problems, or obstacles that must be worked on soon to improve performance. Will have to exert considerable effort to make progress.

Detrimental (49 points and below). Not achieving any progress or results. In a rapidly declining state and is totally or nearly totally hindered from making any progress. Must do something soon. Has very serious problems and, in all probability, will require third-party assistance to overcome them.

The Evaluation Form

It is very important that the manager treat the evaluation form in a highly confidential manner, requiring great sensitivity. Completed forms should be protected and stored in a secure place.

The evaluation form should be forwarded to the employee to complete items 7 through 9, which cover the employee's view of themselves. The employee then returns the form to the reviewing manager.

The evaluation form must be read over carefully so its scope and detail are understood.

Before the evaluation begins, the manager must read the employee's job description to ensure that the evaluation is specific, accurate, and relevant to the job performed, and the employee's self- evaluation (items 7 through 9).

The manager carefully considers the employee's performance during the review period and rates the employee by circling the appropriate value on the rating scale.

Upon completion of the evaluation, the form is set aside for a day or two to allow reflection and assure objectivity. After it is reviewed again by the manager, it may then be presented to the employee.

The Evaluation Interview

The evaluation interview should be conducted in a private location at a pre-arranged time by mutual agreement of the manager and employee. The interview should be conducted with the following guidelines in mind:

- Keep the interview objective, related to facts of performance or affecting performance only. Do not allow personal feelings to intrude.
- Keep the discussion on a professional level. Personal comments are not appropriate.
- Do not allow the employee to control the interview.

The evaluation form is discussed with the employee, and an explanation given as to how each category was rated. Make every effort to see that the employee understands the evaluation procedure. Alleviate any fears the employee may have of the evaluation by emphasizing that the objective is to help him improve his skills and performance. An employee who does not understand the evaluation is less likely to attempt to improve performance.

An employee's strengths must be recognized and good performance reinforced with recognition and praise.

Discussions of weaknesses must be accompanied with positive suggestions for improvement. This counseling is an integral part of the evaluation process, keeping

XYZ CORPORATION, INC
EMPLOYEE PERFORMANCE EVALUATION FORM

Employee Name: _____   Position: _____

Reviewing Manager: _____   Review Date: _____

Executive Reviewer: _____   Reporting
                                            Period: _____

1.   (Circle the point value)

SUPERIOR	EXCELLENT	ADEQUATE	TOLERABLE	INEFFECTIVE	DETRIMENTAL
10	9	8	7	6	5

COMMENTS:
_____
_____
_____
_____
_____
_____ +

2.   (Circle the point value)

SUPERIOR	EXCELLENT	ADEQUATE	TOLERABLE	INEFFECTIVE	DETRIMENTAL
10	9	8	7	6	5

COMMENTS:
_____
_____
_____
_____
_____

Figure 13.2. Employee Evaluation Form — page 1

3. (Circle the point value)

SUPERIOR	EXCELLENT	ADEQUATE	TOLERABLE	INEFFECTIVE	DETRIMENTAL
10	9	8	7	6	5

COMMENTS:

4. (Circle the point value)

SUPERIOR	EXCELLENT	ADEQUATE	TOLERABLE	INEFFECTIVE	DETRIMENTAL
10	9	8	7	6	5

COMMENTS:

Figure 13.2. Employee Evaluation Form — page 2

5.   **(Circle the point value)**

SUPERIOR	EXCELLENT	ADEQUATE	TOLERABLE	INEFFECTIVE	DETRIMENTAL
10	9	8	7	6	5

COMMENTS:

_____
_____
_____
_____
_____
_____

6.   **SPECIFIC WORK CHARACTERISTICS**

Consider overall effort as judged from the following checklist. Circle the point value awarded in each category. Low for those needing attention; Medium if performance meet general expectations; and High for Special Merit

	Low 1	Medium 2	High 3
Aggressively pursues new opportunities	1	2	3
Attempts to expand level of technical ability	1	2	3
Constantly introduces new concepts	1	2	3
Maintains excellent follow through	1	2	3
Able to focus on significant priorities	1	2	3
Adjusts to changing priorities as required	1	2	3
Maintains high level of communication with peers	1	2	3
Provides clear objectives to staff and peers	1	2	3
Constantly working to develop staff and peers	1	2	3
Demonstrates leadership qualities	1	2	3
Demonstrates willingness to take on additional assignments	1	2	3

Note: Employee Complete Items 7-9

(7) What are the major accomplishments of the employee during this reporting period?

(8) What, if any, major problems/difficulties were encountered during this reporting period?

(9) What are the employee's goals for the upcoming 6 months?

Figure 13.2. Employee Evaluation Form — page 3

10.   EMPLOYEE DEVELOPMENT

Discuss actions employee has taken as a result of suggestions made during previous appraisal or other evidence of self-development. Comment on the employee's performance and growth potential.

---

11.   OVERALL EVALUATION   **TOTAL POINTS FROM #1-#6**   **(36 – 83)**

SUPERIOR	EXCELLENT	ADEQUATE	TOLERABLE	INEFFECTIVE	DETRIMENTAL
79-83	75-78	67-74	58-66	50-57	49 & below

12.   EMPLOYEE COMMENTS

The employee should discuss below any comments or areas of disagreement with this evaluation.

13.   SIGNATURE AND ACKNOWLEDGMENT

Employee's Signature: Date:

Manager's Signature: Date:

President Or Dir.   Date:
Signature:

Figure 13.2. Employee Evaluation Form — page 4

in mind that the objective is to help improve the employee's overall performance. Employees are positively reinforced by doing so.

A commitment must be obtained from the employee to improve in areas of weakness. The employee should understand that improvement is expected. In some cases, the manager may determine that the employee needs further training or education.

The employee must be given the opportunity to make comments and should be encouraged to do so. It is important to remember that the interview is a two-way process.

The company president must approve the evaluation before it is presented to the employee.

Both the manager and employee are required to sign the evaluation form upon completion. A signed copy of the evaluation is given to the employee, a copy is sent to the president, and the original becomes a permanent part of the employee's file.

Performance reviews should be followed up with periodic, informal progress reports. The continuous exchanges must go on to identify and correct problems before they grow into bigger problems.

Management Tips for Performance Reviews

1. Do not wait until review time to let your employee know what you expect of them. Let them know promptly what specific goals, standards, and deadlines you expect them to meet, and how you plan to evaluate and reward their performance.

2. Keep a written record of each employee's performance throughout the period so that you can cite specific examples to back up constructive criticisms or comments you make during the review session.

3. Keep the review focused on the particular employee's performance, showing that you are concerned about them and their career.

4. If you make any judgments, keep them to observable behavior and not about general comments and impressions. Even when rating personality or character traits, talk about specific examples of such traits on the job.

5. Poorly performing employees, in most instances, expect a "poor" scoring evaluation. They may actually welcome the opportunity to discuss their performance with you. Encourage the employee to talk and offer solutions when possible. The employee has ownership of the problem; give them

ownership of the solution. You can help them, but it should not be your sole effort. When emotional problems arise, do not get involved in solving them. Your job is to evaluate the employee and help them to become better at their job.

6. If you encounter an angry employee:
    - Stay calm and simply listen. Anger is a result of fear, frustration, and disappointment.
    - Encourage the employee to talk. Be willing to let them talk frankly.
    - If it gets too emotional, stop the evaluation. Let the person know you will reschedule the interview within the next few days, and let them know you are looking forward to sitting down with them in a constructive manner.

7. Problem areas to avoid:
    - **Vagueness.** Do not be vague. The evaluation is important to the employee in terms of both money and self-esteem. Be very specific about what it will take to upgrade each area of the evaluation.
    - **Not enough preparation.** Do your homework; collect as much background material as possible prior to completing the evaluation form. Refer to your written records.
    - **War stories.** Stay away from comments that do not contribute directly and positively to the evaluation process.
    - **Do not talk about yourself.** This is the employee's evaluation not yours.
    - **Keep the evaluation well balanced,** emphasizing both strengths and weaknesses equally if possible.
    - **Avoid comparisons to other employees or yourself.** Concentrate on the individual employee's performance and behavioral traits.

The Compensation Adjustment Process

"Oh boss, what about my salary increase?" are words that strike terror into the hearts of the bravest employer. Who to give increases to and how much they should be can be overwhelming questions. Unless, of course, you are utilizing the salary adjustment process that I am about to teach you. The process to adjust employee's earnings must be as fair and impartial as the evaluation process itself. Never again will there be any question, for yourself or for the employee, as to whether or not the employee has earned a salary increase and how much that increase will be.

Business owners have told me this process has relieved a lot of anxiety on their part. Just implement this process and reap the rewards!

1. The company must achieve its profit goals for there to be any salary adjustments.
2. If the company achieves its profit goals, it will establish a salary adjustment pool equivalent to 3 percent of the gross salaries paid by the company (excluding owners' salaries). The total amount awarded in salary increases cannot exceed the salary adjustment pool.
3. Employees who achieve a Superior rating will receive an annual increase equivalent to 8 percent of their annual salary (excluding overtime and bonuses).
4. Employees who achieve an Excellent rating will receive an annual increase equivalent to 6 percent of their annual salary (excluding overtime and bonuses).
5. Employees who achieve an adequate rating will receive an annual increase equivalent to 3 percent of their annual salary (excluding overtime and bonuses).
6. Employees who achieve any rating lower than Adequate are not eligible for a salary increase.
7. In the event that not all of the salary adjustment pool is utilized, the balance shall revert to the company.
8. In the unlikely event that the salary adjustment pool is not large enough to implement the salary adjustments called for by the plan, each increase will be reduced by an amount equivalent to the percent difference between the salary adjustment pool based upon the 3 percentage and the amount that is the result of the actual salary adjustments based upon the evaluations. For example, let us assume that based upon the 3 percent, the salary adjustment pool should be $45,000, and the results of the evaluations call for annual increases of $49,500 (a shortfall of 9.1 percent). If an individual who earned $18,000 annually received an excellent rating and was entitled to an 8 percent annual increase (or $1,440), that increase would be reduced by 9.1 percent ($131) and would result in an annual increase of $1,309.
9. These increases should be effective in the third pay week of the second month following the close of the year.

Conclusion

The company's most valuable resource is its personnel. A key element in motivating an employee is periodic formal performance evaluations. The evaluation must assess the employee's value to the company in an equitable and objective manner.

An effective evaluation program will indicate the organization's appreciation of good employees and serve as a basis in any decision to eliminate marginal employees. It also serves as the basis for wage and salary increases, which are objective and quantifiable rather than subjective.

CHAPTER 14

Pay Your Way to Recovery

One of the most important business success indicators is whether or not companies reward employees based on individual performance. How you pay your employees has a lot to do with how they perform. Whenever possible, employees should be paid based on their performance. I recognize that it is not possible to pay every employee solely based on performance, but to the extent possible, that should be your goal. Why, you might ask? Because employees perform more effectively when they are in control of how much they earn. And that goes double for salespeople. I can tell you unequivocally that salespeople should always be paid based on performance, and that does not mean just on how much they sell. You have to be very careful here. If a salesperson is selling a product for which they cannot control the selling price, then it would be fine to pay them a commission based upon their sales. You have a very different story if your sales staff can control the selling price and thus impact your gross margin. In this situation, they must be paid a commission based upon a percentage of the gross margin.

I had a client who had been in business for over forty years. The family patriarch had some health issues and was transitioning the leadership of the company to his sons. Now that sounds like a dandy idea—and certainly good for the sons who had been respectfully waiting for their turn to manage the company. Here's the rub. This company sold industrial projects and consequently was very much sales driven. The father, like so many managers of his generation, managed the company in general and the salespeople in particular with an iron fist. In case you're unfamiliar with the iron-fist method, let me give you an example. Early in my career, I worked in the corporate office of a large retail jewelry chain. The president of that company was an older man who certainly had the iron-fist management style down to a science. He was famous for his theatrics, and I personally witnessed him bring more than one grown man to tears. My most vivid recollection goes back to one day when he had been waiting for one of our store managers to return his call. I was sitting in his office. Here is how the conversation went:

President: "Hi, kid (he called everyone "kid"). How are you?"
Manager: "I'm fine, Mr. XXXX."
President: "How's your family, kid?"
Manager: "They're doing fine, Mr. XXXX. Thanks for asking."
President: "How's your health, kid?"
Manager: "Just fine, Mr. XXXX. I appreciate your concern."
President: "Well then, you rotten little *@#*, what the hell is the matter with your sales?"
Manager: (no answer, just a faint sobbing in the background)

Not everyone (fortunately) can manage that way. Going back to the company in transition, the sons certainly could not pull off that type of management style—nor did they want to.

In my client's company, I found that 95 percent of salespeople's compensation was in the form of salaries, with only about 5 percent of their earnings coming from sales bonuses. The company had lost one of its largest customers, and as a result sales were down. To make matters worse, the market was becoming even more competitive and cutthroat, so margins were also down. Do you know what wasn't down? That's right—the salespeople's compensation. I met with the sales force and found a generally unmotivated, lethargic group of employees who were sorry that sales and margins were down, but looked upon their weekly salary as an entitlement. That left me with the problem of how to motivate the sales staff. I presented a plan entitled "It's Your Business" to the owners (this was really addressed to the father, who was the founder of the business). Our goal was to make the sales staff function as if the business were their own. Here is the presentation that I made to the owners:

> Think back to the early days when you started your business. Weren't there days where you were concerned that you couldn't take a paycheck? Didn't that concern, or possibly that fear, inspire you to reach greater heights quicker than you ever thought possible?

> Do you think that your sales representatives feel the same way that you did then? Or are they comfortable that no matter what, they will get a paycheck? After all, that's what the company is for, to provide compensation for them and their families, no matter how low their productivity level may be.

> How unfair this situation is to those sales representatives, to never really allow them to experience the exhilaration resulting from overcoming whatever obstacles their suspects, prospects, or customers may raise, and to actually earn their compensation rather than simply have it given to them.

> There is no question that entrepreneurial individuals, who are driven by a desire to earn their way through the world, operate at a significantly higher level of productivity and have significantly more adrenaline flowing through their bodies than do individuals who are assured that no matter how low the level of production may be, they are "entitled" to a certain compensation level. Where is their adrenaline level? What inspires them to achieve great heights?

> That is where the "It's Your Business" concept comes in. The idea is to let each individual responsible for the creation of sales experience the same drive that the entrepreneur has.

> You may ask how that can be done, considering that you, the entrepreneur, have already gone past the developmental stage of your business. You have already experienced that rush that comes from beating the odds and bringing home a significant paycheck based upon your accomplishments and your willingness to assume risk.

It is, of course, impossible to recreate the early days of your business, where the amount of compensation you were able to take home depended solely upon your ability to make enough revenue in excess of the company's expenses.

It is possible, however, to create an environment in which your sales representatives can operate in a truly entrepreneurial fashion, where the profitability of their area of responsibility can directly affect their earnings. They will, of course, have an advantage over you, in that your company and your market have already been developed—by you.

You, in effect, will say to those sales representatives that they are now solely responsible for their specific area. You will provide the support, and you may even provide an ever-decreasing draw against their earnings. In the final analysis, they will determine their compensation. There is no ceiling as to how much they can earn; there is also no floor as to how little they can earn. It is truly up to them. It's their business.

And that's exactly how I'd explain this sales compensation process to you. Here is how it works.

- Each sales representative is assigned a specific territory.
- A minimum sales goal may be established.
- A minimum gross margin goal may be established.
- You will educate your sales representative as to the direct expenses that ultimately reduce the profit that they generate. These expenses should include payroll taxes, fringe benefits, cell phone expenses, and any other direct selling expenses that they generate and that would not exist if they were not selling in their specific territory.
- It is appropriate to prorate sales support and marketing costs to the territories based upon a percentage of sales method. It will be interesting to know if they will still want a lot of support if they are paying for it.
- Your accounting personnel will produce, on a monthly basis, income statements prepared on a *cash basis* for each sales representative. This assures they are well informed as to the collection status of their accounts. Because they are paid based upon collected profit, they will be much more likely to ensure their customers pay on time.

- The sales representative will earn 40 percent of the net territory profit he or she produces. This percent must be specified and agreed to at the commencement of the program. (The 40 percent is what we arrived at for this client. You will determine what percent is right for your business.)

It may be appropriate to pay a draw (not a salary) at the beginning of the program. This is clearly your decision, and you may decide that a territory or product investment is warranted. If that is the case, it should be clearly understood that this draw will decrease over a predetermined period of time and will ultimately disappear completely. An example may be a new salesperson who receives a draw of $550 per week for the first two months, then a reduction of 25 percent in each of the succeeding four months, until there is no more draw and they are conducting their professional life like an entrepreneur, complete with the risks and rewards.

Will this program appeal to all sales representatives? No, but it will certainly appeal to the employees who truly believe in their ability to provide value to your company and to provide above-average rewards for themselves and for their families. And after all, isn't that really the type of person you want to have selling your products and representing your company?

For this client, we created a mini-income statement for each salesperson that reflected both sales and gross margin. Deductions from gross margin, such as material handling costs, cellular costs, promotional expenses, payroll tax costs, etc. were shown as a deduction from gross margin, and they were paid 40 percent of their territory profit. It's important to be careful in deciding what commission percent you are going to pay. The rule of thumb is, if you are transitioning from a guaranteed salary to a commission structure, you calculate the percent of sales your current sales salaries are and construct your new commission plan so that this percentage will not increase and may actually decrease.

Remember, this is a motivational tool, so you want the reward for outstanding performance to be real. There should be no ceiling. The plan should be constructed so that the more you pay your sales staff, the more money you will make. When that happens, you no longer have to cajole and coerce them to produce; they are driving themselves because of the reward you established. One caution here. The truly professional salesperson will excel in this environment. His sales will increase, and so will his earnings. You must not be resentful of his increased earnings. His earnings are now solely based upon his performance.

I should let you know as a postscript that the transition from salary to commission for this client was successful, but it was not without its casualties. The company did lose one-third of its six-person sales staff (they were not willing to earn their paychecks), but the replacements were fabulous and the company's productivity showed significant improvement.

Let's assume you have decided to have a commission-based plan—or perhaps you are already paying your sales staff based on a commission plan. Does that mean that success is assured? No, unfortunately it takes sales management to bring our sales performance over the goal line. A good friend of mine told me that you cannot manage people, you manage processes. That is certainly true here. Let's talk about the process that you should use to manage your sales force.

The Sales Management Process

This is a vital part of your success strategy. Salespeople need monitoring, redirection, and reinforcement. Don't get me wrong. They won't hug you when you implement this process. On the day that you go live with the Sales Management Process, you will most likely hear moans, groans, and possibly some threats that revolve around quitting. You will most likely hear words like, "Good grief! I won't have time to work with customers anymore, I'll just be filling out these darn forms." But remember, you are the resident adult here, and you have to do what is right regardless of the resistance that you may encounter. Here are the management process and the forms I have found to be extremely effective and recommend you use.

Sales Representatives' Reporting Standards and Instructions

All salespeople are responsible for maintaining and providing their own records, as well as the company's profile sheet enumerating all the basic facts and statistics of a company. This record can be maintained digitally or in hard copy and must be part of the company's permanent record.

In addition, the representative will need to provide to management, on a monthly basis, a prospect list of new accounts that will be on the next months' schedule for development and expansion. The sales representative will also supply management with a proposed weekly schedule of his or her work plan for the upcoming week. This will assist the rep in efficiently working the whole territory and will provide the sales manager with the information needed to plan his or her own schedule. In addition, the salesperson will be mandated to maintain several other reports that will allow the sales manager to ensure that the various required activity levels have been reached. These reports must be e-mailed or delivered to the sales manager for review at the end of every week or at month-end, depending upon the nature of the report.

The formats for these reports have been designed for implementation in hard copy or in digital form, but they must be always available for management to review.

Weekly Activity Plan. This form is used by the sales rep to plan next week's schedule. It reflects both prospecting calls and existing customer calls for each day of the upcoming week. This form should be e-mailed or delivered to the sales manager by the close of business each Friday in order to allow the sales manager to review and comment. It is important that this weekly plan be completed. A sales representative who begins a week without a specific plan (the plan can be modified as conditions dictate) is truly an unguided missile and not very efficient.

Weekly Call Log. This form is prepared by the sales representative as he or she makes sales calls. In effect, it is a daily log of the rep's sales activities. It is e-mailed or delivered to the sales manager at the end of every week. This form can be used to alert the sales manager about any problems or opportunities that may have come up during the work week.

Customer Profile Sheet. This form is filled out by the sales rep every time a suspect becomes a prospect. This is a permanent record and needs to be kept in the customer's file for reference prior to making a call. This form should be e-mailed or delivered to the sales manager at the end of every week.

Cold Call Report. One of these reports is to be filled out daily for each cold call made by the rep. This report will be submitted to the sales manager at the end of the week, along with the Weekly Activity Plan.

Prospect Account Form. This form is submitted by the sales representative at the end of the third week of every month to the sales manager. It includes a list of twenty prospects for the rep's monthly itinerary to try to convert into a customer in the upcoming month. This is the list that will be utilized to increase the customer base of the company and will be a priority for development during the next month's activity.

Monthly Plan and Review. This form is filled out jointly by the sales representatives and the sales manager. The Prior Month Review analysis looks at booked sales, territory profit, collections, and collected territory profit. The sales manager will complete the rows for Sales, Territory Profit, Collections, and Collected Territory Profit. The next page plans and analyzes the sales representative's projections for 30-day, 60-day, and 90-day goals. The goal page should be submitted to the sales manager no later than the twenty-fifth of each month. The sales manager will review each rep's results with him or her, no later than the fifteenth of each month. The reps will use these forms to analyze their progress and to plan their sales effort. The sales manager will review these forms with the sales representative to define what the company can expect in sales, to outline any unresolved issues, and identify any needed support.

Samples of each of these forms are below. If you would like blank digital copies of these forms, just e-mail me at freestuff@profitabilitypartners.com, and I will send them to you.

Compensating Non-Sales Employees for Fun and Profit

Okay, well, maybe *fun* is not in the equation, but salespeople are not the only employees who can be motivated by the way that you pay them. I had a client who was a concrete contractor. His company had been in business for over forty years and over the past three years had lost over a million dollars. They were down and nearly out. In fact, when I arrived at their office, the CEO told me that she really didn't believe there was much that could be done. This was a serious situation. Morale was as low as their bank account. They really didn't understand why they were encountering this problem. After all, as she told me, "We were bidding jobs and winning them." And there was the rub. They were bidding jobs, and they were winning jobs. Unfortunately they had no idea what their real costs were, and, as a result, for every hour they worked, they were losing about $3. We discussed this issue earlier when we discussed the importance of knowing your fully burdened labor costs. (If you will e-mail me at freestuff@profitabilitypartners.com, I will e-mail you the spreadsheet for calculating the fully burdened labor cost.)

The second problem involved their foremen. No, the foremen themselves weren't the problem—but then again, they sort of were. The foremen were salaried employees whose compensation had no relation to the profitability of their jobs. And a good thing, too, because when I got involved with the company, all of their jobs were losing money. If their compensation did depend on their profitability, they would have had to pay the company. It made absolutely no difference to them whether they had forty employees on one of their jobs or four hundred, and it

XYZ Company, Inc.

Sales Representative

Weekly Activity Plan

FOR WEEK ENDING ________

Sunday	Monday	Tuesday	Wednesday	Thursday	Friday	Saturday

Weekly Activity Plan

Figure 14.1. Weekly Activity Plan

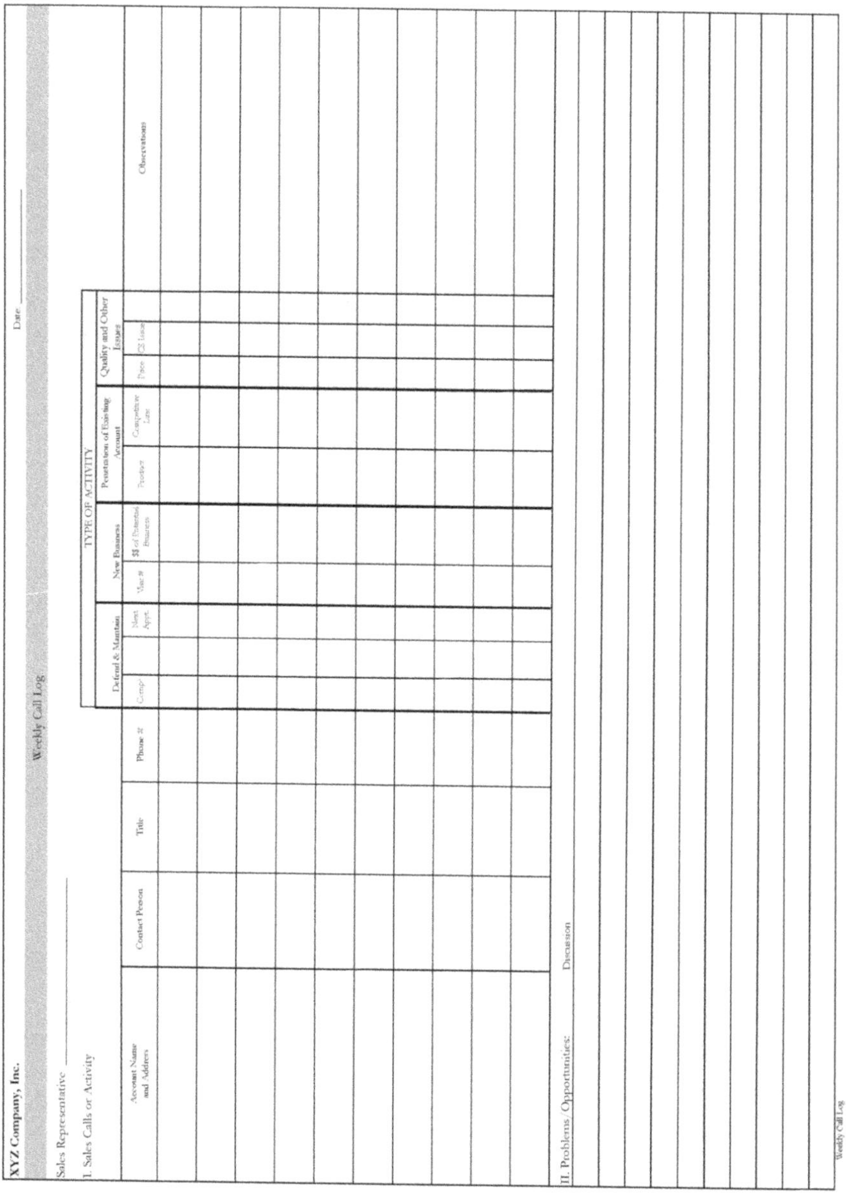

XYZ Company, Inc. Date ____________

Weekly Call Log

Sales Representative ____________

I. Sales Calls or Activity

Account Name and Address	Contact Person	Title	Phone #	TYPE OF ACTIVITY: Defend & Maintain			New Business		Penetration of Existing Account		Quality and Other Issues			Observations
				Comp/		Next Appt.	Visit #	$$ of Potential Business	Product	Competitive Line	Price	CS Issue		

II. Problems/Opportunities: Discussion

Weekly Call Log

Figure 14.2. Weekly Call Log

XYZ Company, Inc.		Date:
	Customer Profile	

Account Type: _____

Name: _____   Primary Contact: _____
Address: _____   Title: _____

Owner's Name: _____

Phone Number: _____   E-mail Address: _____
Fax Number: _____   Website Address: _____

Key Personnel (principals & decision makers):

Name	Title	Responsibilities
_____	_____	_____
_____	_____	_____

Special Characteristics

_____

_____

Number of Employees: _____   Number of Locations: _____

Present Competitors Utilized

Name	Strengths	Weaknesses
_____	_____	_____
_____	_____	_____
_____	_____	_____
_____	_____	_____

Competitors' Products Utilized

_____

_____

_____

How can we get your business? _____

What types of products would you like to see XYZ carry? _____

If new business call, what is the probability of XYZ getting this business? _____

What is the time frame for a decision? _____

Customer Profile

Figure 14.3. Customer Profile Sheet

XYZ Company, Inc.

COLD CALL REPORT

SALESPERSON _____ DATE _____

ACCOUNT NAME:			
STREET:			
CITY:		STATE:	ZIP:
PHONE: ( ) -			
FAX: ( ) -			

TYPE OF BUSINESS
ANNUAL SALES: $

NAME OF PERSON CALLED:
TITLE:
PHONE EXTENSION: (   )   -

DESCRIPTION:

COMMENTS ON CALL:

FOLLOW UP ACTION NEEDED:

FOLLOW UP ACTION TAKEN: DATE

President: _____
Sales Mgr _____

Sales Forms

Figure 14.4. Cold Call Report

XYZ Company, Inc. Prospect Account Form Sales Representative

VI. Top 20 Prospect Accounts:

Account Name and Address	Contact Person	Title	Phone #	Visit #	$$ of Potential Business	Products Interested In
1						
2						
3						
4						
5						
6						
7						
8						
9						
10						
11						
12						
13						
14						
15						
16						
17						
18						
19						
20						

Prospect Account Form

Figure 14.5. Prospect Account Form

XYZ Company, Inc.							Date:	
			Monthly Plan & Review					

Sales Representative _____ for Month of: _____

I. Prior Month Review

A. Sales and Bookings

	Actual	Budget	$ Variance	Y-T-D Actual	Y-T-D Budget	$ Variance
Booked						
Sales			$ -			$ -
Territory Profit $			$ -			$ -
Territory Profit %	#DIV/0!	#DIV/0!	**#DIV/0!**	#DIV/0!	#DIV/0!	**#DIV/0!**
COLLECTIONS						
$ Collected	#REF!	#REF!	**#REF!**	#REF!	#REF!	**#REF!**
Territory Profit Collections	#REF!	#REF!	**#REF!**	#REF!	#REF!	**#REF!**

B. Variance Explanations:

_____

_____

_____

II. Current Month

A. Sales Performance

	Projected	Budget				
# Orders written						
Average Order Written						

C. Attached is my detailed calendar for the month of: _____ (this month)

12/15/2011 Monthly Plan-Pgs 1 & 2

Figure 14.6. Monthly Plan and Review — page 1

XYZ Company, Inc.			Sales Representative:	
Monthly Plan & Review				
Page 2				

III. Next Month - 30 Day Goals:

Activities/Customers	Date	Event	Issues/Support Needed	Value

IV. Two Months Out - 60 Day Goals:

Activities/Customers	Date	Event	Issues/Support Needed	Value

V. Three Months Out - 90 Day Goals:

Activities/Customers	Date	Event	Issues/Support Needed	Value

12/15/2011Monthly Plan-Pgs 1 & 2

Figure 14.6. Monthly Plan and Review — page 2

certainly didn't matter how productive those employees were. In fact, it would not be unusual for the operations manager who controlled staffing to send a concrete worker to a job just to keep him busy, regardless whether the foreman needed him or not. And they never argued when they got an additional employee on their job; after all, how profitable or unprofitable the job was really didn't affect their way of life at all.

I knew that the answer was to get the foremen involved in job profitability in a most personal way. I was going to pay them for controlling the costs on the job. Here is what I did, and it turned out to be a real win-win situation. This incentive program, outlined below, was presented to each foreman.

Foreman Incentive Program

Your incentive plan has been developed to create an atmosphere in which you can earn additional compensation based upon your performance.

In acquiring any work, the company has given a good-faith estimate of the amount of time that will be required to complete the job. Our estimating department has used information readily available to them from industry databases and has added its collective judgment to provide the most competitive and accurate estimate possible.

This estimate, modified by any known variables, will be used for the calculation of any incentive to be earned by you.

The reason for this is simple. The company has been awarded a contract. The basis for the award of the contract was a quote that came directly from the estimate we have created. Consequently, this estimate represents the dollar amount that, absent any change orders and dependent upon the successful completion of the job, the company will ultimately earn on this job. *At the beginning of every job, to ensure that all of the variables have been considered, you will be given the "benchmark hours" upon which your incentive will be based.*

To the extent that there are any change orders, these will be added/deducted from the estimate and the incentive calculation will be adjusted accordingly.

We cannot foresee all circumstances, and often there are adjustments to the amount of money that we will ultimately receive due to modifications to our contract with our customer. Your incentive calculation will reflect these changes.

The purpose of the incentive program is to reward excellence and to pay out of profits.

Unless the company makes a profit, there is simply no extra money available for incentive pay. One of the reasons the program was installed was to in fact assist the company in achieving its profit goals. Also, you have to *earn* the incentive, and to do so you must exhibit exemplary performance that is superior to the ordinary manner in which jobs are managed and supervised. Consequently, the company will not reward "accidents" or "windfalls"—specifically jobs that cause our estimate to be very beneficial to the company. This type of event is rare and will be thoroughly discussed upon its occurrence. Bear in mind that we must give our company owners a certain amount of latitude in dealing with these unusual events.

Prior to the job starting, at the hand-off meeting, you will have the opportunity to review the estimate and put in your own informed judgments as to the time necessary to complete the job. You will not be penalized for informing management before the fact of anticipated problems that are in fact realized.

This is a normal part of our hand-off activity. The important thing to bear in mind is that the purpose of your review of our estimate is to protect us, before the fact, of any items that our estimating group may have missed in their quote. It is critical that we have advance warning of issues. Sometimes we will be able to renegotiate the contract and make ourselves whole. Other times we will all have to work as a team and do the best we can to salvage as much as possible from a difficult situation. Finally, given that you have the right to insulate yourself from risk in the event of a missed estimate on the part of the company, to the extent that you adjust the time required to complete the job upwards and we accept such adjustment, the newly adjusted hours will become the basis for your bonus.

Remember that we have to live with the estimate that we have given our customer. To the extent that we do better than that quote— and make money as a company—excellence will be rewarded.

Here is how you will be able to earn bonus income.

One-Foreman Jobs

If you are able to complete the job in fewer hours than budgeted, you will receive 10 percent of the savings. For the purposes of this plan, each hour will be valued at $17.00. For example, if a job is budgeted for 3,000 hours and you complete the job in 2,700 hours, you will receive 10 percent of the 300 saved hours multiplied by the average hourly rate of $17.00. The bonus in this example would amount to $510.00.

Multi-Foremen Jobs

The hours that each foreman was on the job will be accumulated and the percentage of the total foreman hours will be calculated. For example, if Foreman A spent 100 hours on a job and Foreman B spent 50 hours on a job, Foreman A would have 66.7 percent of the foreman hours and Foreman B would have 33.3 percent of the foreman hours. If the job is completed in fewer hours than budgeted or benchmarked, the foremen who worked on the job will receive 10 percent of the savings prorated by the hours each foreman worked on the job. As above, each hour is valued at $17.00. If a job was budgeted for 4,000 hours and the job was completed in 3,500 hours, the foremen will receive 10 percent of the 500 saved hours multiplied by the $17.00 per hour rate. The savings in this example amounts to $8,500, and the bonus to be spread among the foremen amounts to $850. Foreman A would receive 66.7 percent of the $850, or $567, and Foreman B would receive 33.3 percent, or $283.

Jobs with a Lead Foreman

The hours that each foreman (including the lead foreman) was on the job will be accumulated, and the percentage of the total foreman hours will be calculated. For example, if Foreman A spent 70 hours on a job, Foreman B spent 50 hours on a job, Foreman C spent 30 hours on a job, and the lead foreman spent 100 hours on a job, Foreman A would have 28 percent of the foreman hours, Foreman B would have 20 percent of the foreman hours, Foreman C would have 12 percent of the foreman hours, and the lead foreman would have 40 percent of the foreman hours. If the job is completed in fewer hours than budgeted or benchmarked, the foreman who worked on the job (including the lead foreman) will receive 7 percent of the savings, prorated by the foreman hours worked on the job, and the lead foreman will receive an additional 5 percent of the savings. As above, each hour is valued at $17.00. If a job was budgeted for 10,000 hours and completed in 9,000 hours, the foremen, including the lead foreman, will receive 7 percent of the 1,000 saved hours multiplied by the $17.00 per hour rate. The savings in this example amounts to $17,000, and the 7 percent bonus to be spread among the foremen amounts to $1,190. Foreman A would receive 28 percent of the $1,190, or $333; Foreman B would receive 20 percent, or $238; Foreman C would receive 12 percent, or $143; and the lead foreman would receive 40 percent, or $476. Additionally, the lead foreman would receive a lead bonus of 5 percent of the savings, or an additional $850.

We will pay a portion of the incentive earned at the completion of the job and the balance when the retainage is paid.

The company operates on a different cycle than the particular jobs that we are working on at any one time. Consequently, we have to "hold back" a portion of the payments in order to assure that the company and the foreman share the risk of handling any claims that may occur on a given job through the end of the warranty period. The initial incentive payment will be 60 percent of the total incentive earned. This will be paid upon completion of the final punch list and the Job Completion Checklist. The actual payment will be at the end of the first month following the job completion. The balance will be paid at the end of the first month after retainage has been paid. Please note that this balance may be used to offset the costs incurred on jobs where we had to go back to a job site to do remedial work after the job had been closed. In those cases, you will be charged for 25 percent of the labor charge incurred. Under no circumstances will you ever "owe" the company any money; you may just not receive your total incentive pay if it is offset by jobs that did not benefit anyone.

In order to receive any incentive, you must be an employee of the company, and you must take proper care of tools, equipment, and vehicles.

The office will generate weekly and monthly reports showing your progress on these jobs.

No incentive program is perfect. We have made a good-faith effort to create the best program in the industry for you. If you have any other ideas, remembering that they must benefit both you and the company, let us know. Also, continue to bear in mind that the company is also in the process of creating a pay-for-performance plan, in which every eligible employee will have the opportunity to receive additional compensation if the company exceeds its overall planned profit. Let's make this program a win-win for both the company and for you.

We believe that this is a well-thought-out plan in which both the company and the foremen will benefit from gains in productivity. The company reserves the right to modify this plan should circumstances warrant such change.

How did that work out for the company? Well, we knew that we had won when, during the week after we unveiled the foremen compensation plan, the operations manager sent a couple of workers out to a job, and the foreman sent them back because he didn't want them and didn't need them. Now the foreman was operating like an owner. And isn't that just what you want to happen? This was a win-win deal. The foreman made money, and the company made money. In fact, because of the combination of the company selling their services for the right price and the foremen controlling costs, the company, which lost over $1,000,000 over the past three years, earned $500,000 in the first year and over $1,000,000 in the second year. This is a perfect example of what can happen when you involve your employees and compensate them for great performance. (It also helps when you are charging the correct amount for your services.)

Now Bring Everyone into the Pay-for-Performance World

As you get through this book, you may notice that our salary administration process (which comes from our employee evaluations), our sales commission process, and our foreman productivity bonuses all share a common trait. All of those pay plans relieve owners from having to decide what someone earns or how large a pay increase to give. Take a moment to review the Employee Performance Evaluation Procedure in chapter 13, "The People Side of the Business."

Now I would like to remove another decision that owners often have to make—the dreaded year-end or Christmas bonus amount to give to employees. Notice that I used the word "give" in conjunction with those bonuses, because that is what happens when Christmas or year-end bonuses are awarded based upon the owner's subjective decision. Of course, there are some good feelings that go along with those types of subjective bonuses, which is why so many business owners hold fast to these old non-productive traditions. After all, don't you feel like the Godfather when you distribute those checks and your employees come into your office and, in their own way, stoop and kiss your ring? Oh yeah, the old ego is really stoked now. Life is good, isn't it? Well, perhaps it is, at least as long as everything is okay with the company, and you, as the benevolent dictator that you are, keep stroking those bonus checks. But what if you stop writing those checks or significantly reduce the amount? There will be no ring kissing this year. You most likely won't hear any employee say, "Don't worry, boss. I understand. I know that the company just doesn't have the money this year. We'll all work harder and next year will be better." No, what you will likely hear are comments like, "Where is my bonus?" or "I've worked hard for that bonus, and now you won't give it to me." You will even hear, "That's not fair." How do you feel now? Pretty low.

Here's the problem. When you pay bonuses that are not based upon objective criteria, you are creating an entitlement. Because of your past actions, even the best and most loyal of your employees will expect you to give them "their bonus," and if you don't, you are judged to be a real Scrooge.

So how do you resolve this problem? Well, you could certainly just issue an edict that there will be no more bonuses. Probably won't be great for morale, but you could do it. Or you could institute a true Pay-for-Performance Bonus Plan utilizing the Quantitative Measurement Process and the Employee Performance Evaluation Process described in chapter 13, "The People Side of the Business." Let's take a look at the way I have implemented it for many of my clients:

Objective of Pay-for-Performance Bonus Plan

The goal of the Pay-for-Performance Bonus Plan is to reward performance that contributes to generating residual profits (profits generated as a result of productivity and efficiency improvements) and to reduce costly employee turnover. It is based upon the performance of all employees, in all job functions, working individually and together to improve business performance in critical operational and service areas in order to generate these residual profits.

Benefits

Companies benefit from this process through increasingly profitable operations, due to employees directly participating in increasing the business' performance level.

Employees benefit from being recognized and rewarded for a job well done by monetarily sharing in the improvement of the business' profits.

Procedure

1. Establish a *bonus pool* from profits that are above an established *base-level performance*. (This is your planned profit.)
2. Set up performance criteria and reward structures for all employees.
3. Be sure management creates a positive operational climate through leadership, operating practices, and communications, which encourage a high degree of employee commitment to and participation in the plan.
4. Ensure employee participation with a structure and process that enables all employees to become most involved in identification, resolution, and avoidance of productivity, quality, and service problems. The elimination of these problems will yield increased profits.
5. Create a reward system that shares productivity and profit, above a primary profit base, between the company and its employees. These profits are referred to as residual profits.

Plan Participation

To be eligible to participate in the plan, an employee must be a current employee and have 180 days, or 1,040 hours, of employment with the company in the twelve months immediately prior to the end of the year for which distribution is being made. Exempt personnel are credited with 40 hours per week worked. Employees are credited with 40 hours for each week of paid vacation. No employee is credited with more than 40 hours each week.

Upon the commencement of employment by the company, employees will receive a personal *quantitative measurement sheet,* which sets out their individual goals and measurement standards. Eligible participants will receive a performance evaluation from their supervisor twice each year, at the end of June and at the end of December. The June evaluation is to be used to give the employee feedback as to how they are doing. The December evaluation is to be used to calculate a participants' score prior to the distribution from the bonus pool. A "Tolerable" evaluation is the minimum requirement to permit participation in the program, and performance evaluation scores will be a factor in determining the amount of each participant's distribution from the bonus pool.

Management reserves the right to terminate the eligibility of any employee, and an employee's right to receive an incentive under the plan can be forfeited due to consistent poor performance, serious breach of company policies, safety rules, or serious customer complaints.

Funding of the Bonus Plan

As a true incentive for performance and productivity, this plan is funded only through increases in productivity and quality that contribute to generating residual profits for the company. Residual profits will result when employees work individually and as a team to improve productivity, control costs, increase revenue potential, be quality conscious, and practice safe work habits.

The bonus pool will be funded from residual profits and will be maintained on a cumulative basis. While the percentage of residual profits may be changed annually at the discretion of the president, the available pool for the initial plan year will be 40 percent of residual profits. The calculation of residual profits available for distribution will be based on the excess of profits at the end of the year as compared to the operating plan for the year. Only current employees will be eligible for the year-end distribution. For example, if residual profits (the pre-tax amount earned in excess of planned profits) are $100,000, the amount available for distribution will be $40,000. The pool will be reduced as payments are made to eligible participants.

Allocation of Bonus Funds

Once the bonus pool for distribution has been calculated, the incentive amount available for distribution to each eligible employee will be determined as follows:

The amount to be distributed to each eligible employee will be indexed based upon his or her last Performance Evaluation Rating, as indicated below, before any payments are made.

Performance Evaluation Rating	Modifier Index
Superior	150%
Excellent	125%
Adequate	75%
Tolerable	30%
Less than tolerable	0%

Figure 14.7. Performance Evaluation Rating Table

Bonus Distribution

A distribution from the available bonus pool will be made to all eligible employees annually. Payments will be made on the last payday of the second month following the year-end closing date. This is to give the company an opportunity to get through the year-end financial statement process.

To receive a payout, the individual must be currently employed by the company, employed for a minimum of 180 days during the previous 12 months, have worked 1,040 hours or more during the previous 12 months, and fulfill all of the requirements to participate in the plan.

The following is an example of an annual distribution under the rules of the Pay-for-Performance Plan. As you will see, the bonus pool is distributed to the eligible participants through a two-step process. The first step creates a preliminary distribution in the form of a prorated share based upon the participant's salary. (Please note: many companies distribute the preliminary allocation based upon hours worked.) The final step modifies the preliminary allocation by applying the modification index, which could either increase or decrease the participant's share. Take a look at the example on the next page:

In this example, only $17,094 of the potential $25,000 was paid, thus $7,906 will remain in the pool for potential future distribution.

Conditions for Payment

A pay-for-performance payment will be made only if there is a cumulative year-to-date balance in the pay-for-performance pool.

The ownership of the company may, at their discretion, defer payment of the pay-for-performance incentive if, for any reason, the company's cash balance at payment date is not at least four times the amount to be paid out under the Pay-for-Performance Plan.

Responsibilities

The owners authorize the plan and approve payments to participants. Administration maintains the plan records and reports, administers payouts, and maintains pay-for-performance pool data.

Employee	12-month Earnings	Individual %	Performance Share	Rating	Bonus Modifier	Bonus $
A	$ 42,500	13.6	$ 3,400	Superior	150%	$ 5,100
B	$ 53,100	17.0	$ 4,250	Excellent	125%	$ 5,312
C	$ 36,000	11.5	$ 2,875	Adequate	75%	$ 2,156
D	$ 29,900	9.3	$ 2,325	Adequate	75%	$ 1,744
E	$ 55,000	17.7	$ 4,425	Tolerable	30%	$ 1,327
F	$ 36,000	11.5	$ 2,875	Ineffective	0%	$0
G	$ 60,000	19.4	$ 4,850	Tolerable	30%	$ 1,455
Total	$311,600	100	$25,000			$17,094

Figure 14.8. Annual Employee Distribution of Bonus Pool

Summary

The success of a Pay-for-Performance Plan is based upon management's support of the concept and their ongoing involvement in and recognition of the group participants' achievements. Monetary rewards alone will not result in the desired improvement if management does not treat this program as a high priority. But the real question is, does it work? Well, let me tell you about a client of mine whose employees demonstrated just how well it can work. This was a particularly difficult client. The owner of the manufacturing company was a poor listener and rarely followed through with processes that we installed. He also had a bad reputation with his employees, because poor operating results forced him to stop giving them "their" bonus money at Christmas. Employees had a lot of bad feelings about the discontinuance of this entitlement, and as a result they became uncooperative. This company had a history of many problems on the assembly line and a real absentee problem.

I met with the owner and explained the plan to him. While he liked the concept, he told me that his employees would never buy into the plan. I asked him to humor me and let me explain the plan to the employees and see if we could get a buy in. We did meet with the employees, and while they were a little cynical, they asked great questions and I thought we had a win. So we made the plan official. All of the employees understood that they could only earn bonuses if the company earned more profit than the plan called for. I then went home.

The following week I returned and, as was my custom, went to the owner's office. "Well, did you see any differences in the employees since we installed the plan?" I asked. The owner responded that he would say there was significant difference. He told me that one of the folks on the assembly line made a mistake that resulted in the stoppage of the assembly line. One of his fellow workers threw him up against the wall and told him that he was now in his pocket and affecting his earnings. I can assure you that would not have happened prior to the plan.

This is worthwhile. Make this happen and get your employees involved. You must talk about the plan not only when you implement it, but all year round. Keep the plan on the top of everyone's mind. You will be amazed at the changes that will take place, and you will do away with entitlements.

Note: There is not just one way to make this work. You can alter the amount of profit over and above the operating plan that you are willing to share. In this example, we were sharing 40 percent. Many of my clients share 50 percent. Some of my clients have even established a base dollar amount that is less than the planned profit. This is your call. The important thing is to get this type of a plan implemented. The changes that come about as a result of it can be life changing.

CHAPTER 15

Collect Your Way to Recovery

I f you implement even 75 percent of the processes that you find in this book, you will have taken great steps toward increased profitability. The truth is, however, if you don't collect the money from your sales, your profitability will not matter one bit. I can't tell you how many companies I have seen that have been brought to the point of ruin by bad collection practices. Collections can be difficult, but surprise, surprise! I have a process that will solve the problem for you. If you will implement this and really live it, your delinquency problems will go away. So let's start off by looking at the principles of any good collection process:

- Timely customer invoicing with well-defined payment terms
- Reviewing an accounts receivable aging at least once per week
- Persistent follow-up using standardized collection procedures (I suggest the procedures shown in this section)
- Since payment terms can vary, they should be covered in any written quotation, contract, or invoice. Also, the invoice should state, "Balances

over 30 days past the invoice date are subject to a 1.5 percent monthly service charge."

- Prompt collection of money due to lessen the chance of loss. Statistics show that the older an account becomes, the greater the risk of not collecting and the greater the risk of losing the customer.

The Collection Process

Now let's look at the actual collection process. The process to minimize collection procedures starts at the time that the purchase order or contract is received for a credit sale. If your company is in the construction industry, you must be sure that upon receipt of a purchase order or contract, all steps are completed to ensure that the appropriate Notices to Owners are filed within the time frame required under the laws of the state in which you are performing the work. Other industries don't have to deal with that step.

The collection procedure begins with the invoice. At this time all the appropriate information (customer name, address, telephone number, pricing, and terms) must be recorded. Verification that existing customers have a current status (less than sixty days past due) must be completed. If the customer does not have a current status, management must authorize the delivery of any service or product to that customer, and the decision to service that customer must be made very judiciously.

Prompt invoicing is the next essential element. All invoices should be sent out at the earliest possible date. It is imperative that you be able to identify customer problems before the invoice is due, whenever possible. The delays and bad customer relations that result from asking for payment on an invoice that has been incorrectly priced or for a product or service that was unacceptable (in the customer's view) not only wastes time, it costs money. So the first call should be made fourteen days after the invoice was sent to the customer. Here is an example of what the call should sound like:

"This is Cheryl from XYZ Company. I am calling to make sure that you have received our invoice #---------, and to make sure that the invoice was correct and that you were satisfied with the work that we did for you (or the product that you purchased from us)."

Now pause and wait for a response. If the customer has a complaint with the service provided, the price charged, or for whatever reason does not have the invoice, address this situation immediately. If, for some reason, the customer does not have the invoice, see if one can be faxed or e-mailed that day. If the invoice has been received and no problems exist that would delay payment, simply respond:

"Thank you, we appreciate your business. I'll indicate on my records that everything is in good shape and we can expect payment on the _____ (due date)." Pause again and wait for the response. The pause is vital. The customer must respond in order for you to get a true picture of the situation.

If the response is that they cannot pay until they receive a certain payment, ask when they expect payment and get a commitment as to the date that they project that payment will be made.

This call should be made to eliminate delays that cause delinquency. The sooner you receive a commitment to be paid, the less likely it will become a collection problem.

Addressing Common Excuses for Nonpayment

In reality, there are only a limited number of excuses you will hear regarding an invoice that has not been paid. The designated person(s) responsible for collection must be aware of the frequently used reasons, valid or invalid, and be prepared to respond to the excuse and make the collection. The following list accounts for approximately 90 percent of the excuses used:

- The product was not adequate.
- The invoice was not received.
- The invoice was not correct— e.g., overcharged.
- We don't have the money.
- We have paid the invoice, or the check is in the mail.
- We have not been paid yet. (This is common for construction-related companies.)

The product or service was not adequate.

Determine the nature of the problem and make arrangements for the appropriate employee to have the problem investigated, corrected, or resolved. This communication should be recorded on a copy of the invoice, appropriately marked with comments, and given to the appropriate employee and noted for follow up. After being notified that the problem is resolved, the employee calls the customer and confirms that the problem was corrected to their satisfaction. A firm commitment for payment is then established. Without prior company approval, the individual responsible for collecting accounts receivable should never negotiate reduction in the invoice to secure payment.

The invoice was not correct.

Handle as above.

We don't have the money.

Ask when they will have it. Get a definite commitment for the date when a check will be mailed. Make a note of it and call that day to confirm that the check has been mailed. Make a note of the check number and amount.

The invoice was not received. (Maybe we lost it.)

Verify to whom the invoice copy should be mailed, and the address. Ask if you can fax or e-mail the invoice to them today. If yes, when will they make payment? If no, mail copies to that individual and follow-up in five days to verify receipt of the duplicate invoice and get a commitment for payment.

We have not been paid yet—how can we pay you? (And they don't have "pay when paid" clause.)

If their purchase order or contract does not specify "pay when paid," remind them politely that their purchase order indicates that they would pay us per terms and not when they get paid. Ask what it would take to get our invoice processed for payment. If it becomes obvious that you will have to wait until they are paid, ask, "When do you expect payment?" Make a note of that date and call them back on that date. Ask if payment has been received, and if it has, say, "Thank you. What day will our payment be issued?" Wait for a response, make a note of the date, and thank them.

It may be necessary at times, especially in construction-related situations, to call the owner and verify whether or not the contractor has received payment.

We have paid the invoice, or the check is in the mail.

Get the check number, amount, and date mailed. If the check has been in the mail for more than seven days, request that the customer stop payment and issue another check.

Regardless of the excuses given, the purpose of the contact with the customer is to get a commitment for payment and collect moneys while keeping the customer satisfied.

I Would Rather Write a Letter

From time to time, you will find that one of your collectors would prefer to write collection letters rather than make a telephone call. This is usually a sign that the collector is adverse to confrontation. If a collector is confrontation adverse, he may be in the wrong job. The question is, why is it better use the telephone? Primarily because your customer may have valid reasons why he or she has not paid an invoice. Letters will not reveal reasons or identify any problems. A letter will not let you hear the tone of the customer's voice. Telephone calls are less expensive and give a more personal touch. Telephone contact is faster, more effective, and brings you into direct contact should there be a problem.

By asking the proper questions over the telephone, the collector will be able to determine the problem and provide a quick resolution. Remember, Alexander Graham Bell invented the best collection tool ever. Be sure your folk are comfortable using it.

As you follow the entire collection process, including the fourteen-day calls, it is essential that you maintain a documented history of the steps taken, commitments made, and other pertinent data. Every collection contact must be noted in the diary function in the accounting system (almost every accounting system today has some sort of note capability), along with the appropriate date and the initials of the person making the collection contact. It will also serve as key documentation should you have to go to court in order to collect. Use your system-based reminder system to notify you of your next key dates.

At times, it may be advisable to confirm verbal (telephone) commitments made by the customer in writing (fax/e-mail). This can be done as follows:

Dear Mr./Ms. _____,

We are writing to confirm our conversation today _____ (date). You promised to pay on our invoice number _____ in the amount of $_____ on _____ (date). We want to thank you for your business and assure you that we will always do everything within our power to provide you with extremely high-quality services and products.

When the Account Is Delinquent

Until now, we have only talked about the fourteen-day call, which is certainly a proactive approach to collections. Now let's talk about the collection process when the fourteen-day call didn't work, and we now have a delinquent account.

It is easy to get sidetracked in a telephone conversation unless you follow a guide. The steps outlined below have proven effective. *Be sure you develop a working relationship with someone who can make a decision.*

The philosophy is very much the same as in the fourteen-day call, in that silence is truly golden. You will again ask a question and wait for a response, even if you have to wait over a minute. The customer must commit themselves. The typical collector will say something like, "Okay, Mr. Customer, I see that you owe us over $1,000. Do you think you could have that to us by the end of the month?" The customer says something like, "I'll try," and the collector makes his next ineffective collection call. The effective collector makes his call the first day the account goes delinquent and has a conversation that goes something like this:

Identify yourself and your company. "This is _____ with XYZ Company, and I am calling regarding our invoices of _____ that our records indicate is past due."

At this point pause and wait for a reply. Even if the pause lasts thirty seconds, wait for a reply. Get all of the facts, overcome all objections, and get a commitment for payment.

Be sure to document the call. Record your notes, with date stamped in the accounting system diary function, and update all applicable records.

Of course, even though they promised to pay on a certain date, some of them will actually have lied to you. Imagine that! Use the diary and reminder function in the accounting system to be sure a payment date is not missed. So now a follow-up call is warranted, and here is how it should go:

Identify yourself and say,

"On_____ (date) you promised me that you would send payment in the amount of $_____. We have not received the check." (Pause and wait for a reply, no matter how long the pause.)

If they have not mailed the check, determine why. Get another promise and inform the person that you will call that day to get the check number, or someone will stop by and pick it up, if it is geographically convenient.

Remember, past-due customers are people. Always treat them courteously and with respect while collecting money.

Once the account reaches past sixty days, the CEO should be notified to determine whether to stop any further credit sales to the customer and whether legal action should be taken. At this time, a decision must be made as to how long to wait before legal or other collection action will begin. It is imperative that folk in the construction industry remain knowledgeable regarding lien laws or bond claim requirements, so that you do not miss a due date or fail to comply with a mailing or notice requirement. In any event, the collector must be sure that all timing requirements regarding lien laws (if applicable) are met and that your interests are protected.

When the collection efforts have failed, a formal letter should be sent to the account. Here you are serving formal notice that unless payment is received within a certain number of days, the account will be turned over to a third party for collection. (Or that, in the case of a construction company on a bonded job, you intend to make a claim to their bonding company and to lien the job.)

It should be noted that whatever decision has been made at this time, the company must face the reality of losing a customer and any uncollected asset.

Remember, the more persistent and proactive you are in conducting the steps described earlier, the less likely the company will be in the position of being forced to take third-party action.

I shouldn't leave the subject of collections without discussing the possibility of a personal visit. That type of action can occasionally be effective. I recently spent some time with the CEO of one of my clients. They had a customer who operated a nail salon and had owed them several thousand dollars. They had stopped lying to the collector and had begun hanging up when she called. We were about at the point of filing a lawsuit in small claims court, but the CEO decided to try one more thing. We walked into the nail salon and asked for the owner. She identified herself. (There were several customers in the salon at the time.) The CEO told her who he was and that he had come to collect the money that was due him. She actually had only two choices. She could pay him, or she could let her customers know that she was a deadbeat. She went over to the front desk and reluctantly wrote him a check. We obviously made a mad dash to her bank to trade her check for a cashier's check before she had a chance to stop payment on the check, which I am sure was her intent. So this is an option. It won't work every time, but if you catch the owner of the debtor in exactly the right position (that is, in front of his customers), it can pay dividends.

Take advantage of your small claims or magistrate courts in your locality. Here you can represent yourself and save significant legal costs. You do have to have your ducks in a row and know the rules of the court. There are also limits as to the value of the cases that you can file, which typically range from $5,000 to $15,000 or more.

Alert! In the early stages of this process, you will encounter customer reactions that range from surprise to anger. This is to be expected. You have trained some of your customers to believe that it is acceptable for them to pay you at their convenience. In truth, this is not at all acceptable and is potentially damaging to your company. You have provided a quality product that the customer needed, and now we are simply asking for your money. Note that the operative word is "your money." You will have to deal effectively with the resulting culture shock. You must find a way to communicate to your customers that while you do value their business, it is imperative that the company be paid within your payment terms so that it can continue to provide the quality products and services that they depend upon.

Measuring Your Collection Efforts

Now that you know the correct collection process, and you are committed to helping your cash flow by improving collections, how will you measure your collection efforts? Well, the uninformed business owner (the one that has not read this book) will simply look at the accounts receivable aging report and say to himself, "Receivables over 90 days old are $500,000, and that is down from last month. We are doing well." That is just not an effective way to judge your collection efforts. The fact that 90 days and older receivables are down to $500,000 may signify a victory—or it may not. The real way to measure your results is by calculating the average number of day's sales in accounts receivable. It's an easy calculation. You total up your sales for the past 90 days and divide that number by 90 to get the average daily sales. You then divide that average daily sales into the accounts receivable to get the average number of days of sales that you have tied up in accounts receivable. If your terms are net 30, you shouldn't have much more than 30 days of sales in your accounts receivable.

For example, let's say Company XYZ's total sales for the past 90 days are $540,000. So $540,000 divided by 90 equals average daily sales of $6,000. The total accounts receivable is $240,000. $240,000 divided by $6,000 equals 40 days of sales in accounts receivable. So by looking at that calculation and assuming that 30 days is your goal, you know that you are over by 10 days, which means that you have $60,000 more in receivables and less in cash than you should have.

If you use this process and this measurement, you will truly be managing your receivables in a professional manner and will be maximizing your cash flow. As the saying goes, "Cash is king." Your delinquent customers have your cash. Now go get your money and remember that a non- paying customer is of no benefit to you.

Afterword

So now we've come to the end of our journey. Well, actually, that isn't exactly the truth. What we have come to is the beginning of *your* journey, as now it is your job to begin actually using the processes that we have discussed here.

Granted, some of the processes are more difficult than others, and some of the processes require that you change the very way that you manage your business. But isn't change what you were looking for when you bought this book? Don't you want to be able to sleep nights again without worrying about whether or not your business will survive, or will do more than just barely get by?

Let's get busy and start the process. Change won't happen quickly, and it won't happen easily, but given your commitment to make real changes in your business and your determination to stick with it no matter how much resistance you get from your employees, it will happen.

You will wind up with a business that is effectively managed, profitable, and cash positive, and that has customers who are totally committed to doing business only with you.

You may have questions. Feel free to contact me at sandy@profitabilitypartners. com, and I will try to answer your questions. If it takes more than a quick e-mail, we may need to arrange some telephone consultation. The important thing is to let nothing stand in the way of your commitment to change. These changes will benefit your own well-being, your family's well-being, your employees' well-being, and your customer's perception of your company. I hope that this book helps you improve your life by improving your business. If it has, please send me an e-mail and let me know. Good luck!

About the Author

Sandy Steinman is a Connecticut native but grew up in Tennessee. For the last twenty-seven years he has resided in Jacksonville, Florida.

Sandy received his undergraduate degree in business from the University of Miami in Coral Gables, Florida and completed his MBA work at Southern Methodist University in Dallas, Texas.

He spent much of his career in C-level positions for both public and private corporations. Much of his time was spent in turning troubled companies around.

He spent several years as senior consultant for a large national consulting company specializing in small- and medium-sized troubled businesses, and he ultimately founded and became president of Profitability Partners, Inc., a Florida-based consulting company specializing in the turnaround of small- and medium-sized businesses.

In all, Sandy has enabled millions of dollars in additional profits for his client companies over the years and has literally changed the lives of many of the owners of those businesses.

Printed in the USA
CPSIA information can be obtained
at www.ICGtesting.com
JSHW022335140824
68134JS00019B/1497